Scoring Stocks

2nd Edition

Tony Pow

Why you invest

You need to learn about investing sooner or later in your life. You need to take some calculated risks. Compare the returns of the following assets: cash, CDs, treasury bills, bonds, real estate and stocks. We start with the risk-free investments and end with the riskiest. It turns out that the average returns are in the opposite order. Cash and CDs are not risk-free as inflation eats our profits. For example, the real return is negative for the 2% return in a CD and a 3% inflation rate. In addition you have to pay taxes for the 'returns'. Our capitalist system punishes us for not taking risk.

There are two kinds of risk: blind risk and calculated risk. If you buy a stock due to a recommendation from a commentator on TV or a tip, most likely you are taking a blind risk. It would be the same in buying a house without thoroughly evaluating the house and its neighborhood. When you buy stocks with a proven strategy (i.e. when/what stocks to buy and when/what stocks to sell), you are taking a calculated risk. In the long run, stocks with calculated and educated risks are profitable.

Be a turtle investor by investing in value stocks and holding for longer time periods (a year or more). "Buy and Monitor" is better an approach than "Buy and Hold" as some could lose all the stock values such as in the failure of Enron.

For experienced investors, shorting, short-term trading and covered calls would make you good profits. Simple market timing would reduce your losses during market down turns. If you buy a market ETF and use my simple market timing, you should have beaten the market by a wide margin from 2000 to 2019.

With so many frauds and poor management, do not trust anyone with your investing. Do not buy investing instruments that are highly marketed such as annuity and term insurance.

If you are a handy man and do not mind to satisfy the constant requests of your tenants, buy real estate in growing areas could be very profitable in the long run. Take advantage of the tax laws such as investing in a 401K especially the part that is matched by your company and/or a Roth IRA.

Why you want to read this book

It should improve your financial health substantially. There are about a million investment books. Why we need another one?

- I select proven ideas from more than 100 books besides my original ideas and experiences. I also include links to current articles that will bring more depth to the topic. It is not a novel or documenting the story of my life. All related chapters are grouped in a section for easy future reference. Some chapters are not easy to digest as they have a lot of pointers and some may require you to try them out yourself.

- My friend and I were making similar incomes. I retired 10 years earlier than he and I had more than 4 times he had. Following the right screens that have proven recently is a good reason.

- A best seller was written by a young writer whose main income was from his books and none from his investing. His book is good for beginners or you want to brush up your English. Most of my incomes are from investing.

- Many popular books claiming the authors making millions. However, usually their techniques are hard to follow. Many admitted they had been bankrupted many times. Hence, their chance of bankrupting again is very high. Is bankruptcy fine with you? I cannot afford bankruptcy past and present. My techniques minimize risking my money.

- There are many popular books. They worked very well at one time and folks making millions following the advices. However, look at their recent performances of the last five years. Most of them cannot even beat the S&P 500 index.

- Watch out reviews that are written by friends. As of 8/2015 I do not know any of reviewers on my books. Check out my success stories.
- Why you want to invest? Our capitalist system punishes us for not taking risk. To illustrate, 50 years ago you had a choice not to invest your $10,000, invest it in the stock market or buy real estate. Your buying power of your cash is eaten by inflation. Most likely the other choices beat inflation by huge margins.

Contents

Amazing returns

To achieve a consistent 10% return above S&P 500 over many years is every fund manager's dream. To double one's investment above the S&P500 return is amazing while tripling it is unheard of. I beat the S&P500 by 700% and I can detail the history of my transactions.

Many analysts show their average yearly returns and/or their returns of their top 10 stocks this time of year. The market has closed early today on Christmas Eve, so I have the time to check my recent performance. As a trader with many trades, it would be far too complicated for me to do the same for the entire year. I selected all the stocks I purchased in the last 90 days. Most of them are deeply-valued stocks. Let's check how I performed so far on these stocks.

Whenever you have achieved a high return such as this one, take the profit as it may have reached its peaks. To me, most profits are made in swing trades with an average holding period of just 90 days.

Stocks bought and their returns as of 12/25/12

Stocks	Date Bought	Return	SPY Return
BANR	12/07/12	3%	-.13%
KTCC	12/06/12	0%	.7%
QCOR	12/07/12	15%	-.1%
KTCC	12/06/12	-1%	.7%
ACTV	12/05/12	-5%	.7%
IAG	12/05/12	-1%	.7%
ADES	12/04/12	6%	.6%
NC	12/03/12	15%	-.3%
VELT	12/03/12	64%	-.3%
ANR	11/28/12	33%	4.8%
AAPL	11/16/12	1%	4.8%
C	11/14/12	13%	3.0%
DECK	11/13/12	16%	2.7%
MSFT	11/13/12	0%	2.7%
ALU	11/13/12	38%	2.7%
DLTR	11/09/12	7%	3.4%
CAT	11/08/12	4%	1.9%
MSFT	11/07/12	-8%	.5%
BSX	10/24/12	14%	.3%
BSX	10/19/12	7%	.3%
20			
AVG:		11%	1.35%

Beat SPY (in %) = (11%-1.35%)/1.35% = 716% or 7 times

Average Return = averaging each return of 20 stocks = 11%
Average Annualized Return = 148% or 122% (= 11% *365 / avg. holding period)
Average Return = Profit / Capitalization   = 10%[1]

How the returns are calculated

Using BANR to illustrate how the return and the SPY return are calculated.

BANR	12/07/12	3%	-.13%

BANR was bought on 12/07/12 (17 days from 12/24/12) at 27.93 and it was at 30.43 on 12/24/12.
Rate of Return = (30.43 – 27.93) / 27.93 = 3%

SPY was at 142.53 on 12/07/12 and at 142.35 on 12/24/12.
  Rate of Return = (142.35-142.53) / 142.53 = -.13%

Commissions and dividends are not included for simplicity. Commissions are negligible and dividends could add about another 2% for the annual returns.

Interpreting the performance results

The quantity of each stock bought is not important as I am comparing the return of the stock. However, a few stocks have been listed twice as I bought two times usually on separate dates. If I chose them as one purchase instead of two, my return would appear even better. The purchases are real, so the amount of each stock is not identical to each other.

I'm not too excited yet. This phenomenal return could be just this one time only. 90 days is a short period. Consistency could be achieved with an improved stock picking technique, plain luck or a combination. By any measure, it is an extremely decent return. However, I do not expect beating S&P 500 by 7 times again.

My best return is from 2009 in my largest taxable account. It was over 80% beating the SPY by about 3 times. 2003 is another good year for profit. These two years are defined by me as the Early Recovery stage in a market cycle and the market provides the best profit opportunity.

The four losers are MSFT (-8%), ACTV (-5%), KTCC (-1%) and IAG (-1%). The best winners are: VELT (64%), ALU (38%), ANR (33%) and QCOR (19%). The following are in a 14% to 16% range: DECK, NC and BSX (2 purchases). Click here for the entire list.

Cheating the results

I could 'cheat' for better results by doing the following, but I did not:

1. Exclude stocks only purchased in last 20 days (instead of 15).

2. If my purchases of CSCO were included, the result would be even better. CSCO has been bought three times on 7/24/12 and it has gained 31% as of 12/25/12. I still have CSCO, but it is not included as it just hit the 90-days requirement.

3. I could include those buy orders that had not been executed due to their fast appreciation.

Hence, there are many ways to cheat, so you should read others' results carefully.

What stocks were included

There were 20 purchases. I bought some stocks twice and that counted as two purchases. None of the stocks have been sold as of 12/25/12. I have excluded the stocks that I am testing a strategy by trading them every month and most are in a separate account.

How the stocks were picked

The majority of the stocks were screened by my selected screens that had been proven profitable in the last 3 to 6 months, or are historically profitable at this stage of the market cycle. I also analyzed most of the screened stocks and assigned a score (15 and higher is a buy) based on the metrics that had a reliable predication recently. I do not stick with the scoring system 100% of the time, but most of them stocks that I purchased twice have high scores.

The poor performers were scored as: MSFT with a score of 13, ACTV 16, KTCC 27 and IAG 23. The scoring system is OK. MSFT should not be bought judging from its low score. However, I believe MSFT has a long-term appreciation potential. The other three are the latest purchases in this portfolio and they may perform better in a longer period of time.

The winners were scored as: VELT 34, ALU was not scored, ANR was not scored and QCOR 30. The scoring system is great for this group. ALU and ANR were selected from two Seeking Alpha articles and their selections were not based on these scores. I read several Wall Street Journal articles on ALU and CSCO to convince myself to buy both of them.

The average winners were scored as follows: DECK 9, NC 26 and BSX was not scored. DECK was selected based on an article from Seeking Alpha and it seemed DECK was experiencing the same short squeeze as CROX once did. BSX was selected from a Sunday paper article.

Observations

1. I notice that most big winners (ALU is $1) have a stock price less than $10. The myth of holding quality stocks with prices higher than $15 is not true here as most of my big winners were below $10 including ALU.

2. I did not double my normal purchases on VELT and ALU, which both turned out to be my best performers. VELT scored high in my analysis. ALU was very convincing but it seemed to be risky. 'Nothing risk and nothing gained' applies here. I did triple my purchase on CSCO, which is a large company with good fundamentals that were not yet 'discovered' by the market.

   Both AAPL and DECK gained more than 25% and then lost most of their gains during my short holding period. I should have sold AAPL as many of my fellow investors sold the winners expecting higher capital gains taxes next year. The myth of 'buy and hold' does not work here.

3. During this period, I had several buy orders that were not executed due to their rising stock prices. Market orders could be the solution. It is another example of pennies smart and a pound foolish.

4. It will be interesting to check the results again in 6 and 12 months. Except ALU, all are in my taxable accounts and I usually keep them for a year to qualify for the lower tax rates due to capital gains.

5. I have not described any specific method, but these concepts help you to build better strategies to customize to your individual situations and/or market conditions. Invest the money you can afford to lose. Past performance does not guarantee future results.

6. Reading articles such as Seeking Alpha can be beneficial providing they are not 'bump-and-switch' scheme. However, you should do your own analysis. It is your money after all.

7. The market has been up by .8% in the last 90 days and this portfolio increased by 11%. If my portfolio amplifies the market, I wonder whether it will be down by the same rate in a down market.

8. This portfolio is quite diversified even that I have not planned that way except weighing more with high tech companies. There are no big winners and no big losers that could change the average returns.

9. I tried not to include emerging countries such as China as I do not trust their balance sheets.

10. I have never achieved such an amazing return. I'm emotionally detached to big wins and big losses. It could be plain luck. Even the best strategy will have its "black swan" moment eventually.

11. To achieve over 100% annualized return is not sustainable by checking the top performers of the S&P 500 index and their returns. However, it is possible but not likely if you churn your portfolio more than once and you time the market correctly.

12. Time to take profits as most stocks here have achieved my objectives. Use the cash to buy stocks with a similar appreciation potential. You will never go broke taking profits.

Conclusion

My three steps of making a stock purchase are: 1. Market timing, 2. Screening stocks, 3. Stock Analysis and 4. When and what to sell. They have all been discussed throughout the book. Market timing and strategy (#2 and #3) does not always work, but it will go better with using them.

I am the living proof *against* the Efficiency Theory and the claims that stock picking does not work. It may not work from time to time, but in the long run it works.

Footnote

[1] Profit / Capitalization should be a little less than 20%. The original 10% is correct when you invest all the 20 stocks at the start of the beginning of the investment period. I bought these stocks on different dates. If I assume the average time of all the stock purchases is at a mid-point, then my average capitalization is only half and hence giving a 20% return.

It is slightly less than 20% as I did not include the stocks that I bought in the last 15 days. Use the number for a comparison and that's why we have to be concerned with the performance from most investment subscriptions.

Introduction

Enter the fundamental metric information such as P/E for any 100 stocks into a scoring system. If the top 25% of the stocks perform a lot better than the rest in 6 months consistently, then it is a good scoring system.

I have been using my own scoring system for years. It sums up the individual scores for selected fundamental metrics. When the total score passes a set number, I evaluate the stocks further for potential purchase. This scoring system has been updated many times for refinements and adapting to the changing market conditions. All basic metric information can be obtained from free websites.

Many companies and academic projects must have worked on this kind of stock scoring systems. However, few if any can prove their systems work consistently.

I may have found the reason why it does not work consistently. The fundamental metrics change when market conditions change. To illustrate, the current market conditions may favor value stocks while some other conditions favor growth stocks. I monitor the performances of all the fundamental metrics periodically and make changes accordingly. Hence, I call my scoring system Adaptive Stock Scoring System (do not use the acronym).

In writing this book, I switched the illustrative example from IBM to Apple IBM scored very low. Apple scored very high. This book was published in 06/2013. The performance of the two stocks from 06/03/2013 to 06/03/2014 are as follows:

Stock	Return
IBM	-12%
Apple	41%
SPY (for comparison)	17%

Adaptive Stock Scoring System is a sample scoring system. Don't be fooled by how it is so simple to use. It is backed up by years of data from real-life trades and refinements. The recent tweaking adapts the system to current market conditions. The data can be obtained from many sources. The rest of the book contains background information.

How this book is used

Most graphs and tables are in landscape orientation (recommended for small screens) for both paperback and e-readers. Some graphs may not be displayed adequately on a small screen of an e-reader. E-readers may be available in the current version of Windows, so you can read e-books on the larger screen of your PC. For better orientation, just flip the e-readers 90 degrees. Some reader lets you select a table or a graph to display it to fit the screen.

A link is usually included for the most screens. Copy it to your browser to display the graphs on your PC if desirable. Instructions on how to produce some graphs are provided as you should try them out. One example is how to produce a chart on detecting market crashes.

The **font size** (Ctrl Minus for browser implementation of e-readers) and line spacing of most e-book formats can be adjusted. The unknown, special character is the "smiling face" that the current Kindle does not convert correctly as of this writing.

There are clickable links to web articles. Most of them are from my own web sites and public web sites such as Wikipedia. Some public links may not be available in the future as they are not under my control and my book offerings may change.

These links extend the usefulness of this book by making available specific topics that may not be interesting to every reader. It also provides articles (most are not written by me) for more in-depth analyzes.

Fidelity Video provides video clips to explain some basic terms and it may require Fidelity customers to sign on in order to view them. Check the trial offer from Fidelity. YouTube offers similar video lessons.

The current version provides most of the links the paperback readers can enter into your browser. Get the same information by entering a search in Wikipedia such as Dogs of Dow.

Investopedia is another source beside Wikipedia.
http://www.investopedia.com/

'Afterthoughts' includes my additional comments and ideas of minor importance.

There are fillers with tips, refreshing pictures (taken by me) and jokes (most original) to fill up the empty space of the printed book. Fillers, links and afterthoughts may disrupt the flow of reading this book. However, no readers so far ask me to take them out even in the digitized version of this book. Many page breaks have been eliminated to improve the flow of the book.

For convenience, this book uses SPY, an Exchange Traded Fund (ETF) simulating the S&P 500, as the benchmark for the market.

Annualized returns (Return * 365 / (Days between)) are used where appropriate for more meaningful comparison. To illustrate, I have a 10% return in 6 months, a 10% in a year and a 10% in 2 years. It is more meaningful to use annualized returns of 20%, 10% and 5% respectively in this example.

Usually I do not include the dividend, so you can add an estimated 1.5% to the annualized return. In addition, compound interest is not used for easier calculation, so the actual return could be even better. Many of my tests are not detailed in this book but their summaries are. It reduces the size of this book that is already huge.

There are not many books on this topic as there is no proven way to score stocks consistently. That is why our scoring system has to be 'adaptive'. It means you have to change the scoring periodically (6 months preferred). I do it once a year. For example, the Blue Chip Growth described here is quite good in prediction. Add them to your score. If you have a scoring system, compare it to the one described in this book.

About the author
I graduated from Cal. State University at San Jose in Industrial Engineering and University of Mass. in Amherst with a MS in Industrial Engineering. My last job was in IT. I have been an investor for over 30 years.
My articles in SeekingAlpha.com.
Click the link (http://seekingalpha.com/author/tony-pow/articles).

Dedication
I sincerely hope this book will build bridges with my fellow investors to exchange information.

Acknowledgement.
Thanks to Wikipedia, SeekingAlpha, Yahoo!Finance and Investopia for the many helpful links to enrich this book.

Important notices
© 2013-2022 Tony Pow. Email to pow_tony@yahoo.com.
No material of this book can be disclosed without the written letter from the author.

Version	Paperback	Kindle
1.0	06/13	06/13
2.0	09/15	09/15
3.5	11/21	11/21

Book store managers can order this book from Createspace.com.
https://tonyp4idea.blogspot.com/2020/12/book-managers.html
Book update.

Section I: ASSS, Adaptive Stock Scoring System

1 Adaptive Stock Scoring System

It also applies to sector investing.

No.	Metric	Good	Bad	Score
1	P/E (use expected P/E if available)[6]	Between 2.5 and 12.5, Score = 2	> 50 or =< 0, Score = -1	
2	Price / Free Cash Flow	< 12, Score = 1	>30 or < 0, Score = -1	
3	Price / Sales[1]	< 0.8, Score = 1	< 0, Score = -1	
4	Price / Book[1]	< 1, Score = 1	< 0, Score = -1	
5	Analyst's Opinion[2]	> 7, Score = 1	< 4, Score = -1	
6	Short % (check reason for high %)	Between 30% & 40%, Score = 1[4]	Between 10% & 20%, Score = -1	
7	Insider Purchase[3]	Score = 1		
8	Profit Margin[3]	> 25%, Score = 1	< 5%, Score = -1	
	Compare Q to Q last year for #9 and # 10			
9	Revenue Growth[3]	> 15%, Score = 1	< 0, Score = -1	
10	Earning Growth[3]	> 20% , Score = 1	< 0, Score = -1	
11	Intangibles	Positive, Score = 1	Negative, Score = -1	
			Grand Score	
	Stock Symbol Date[5]	Current Price	SPY	

Footnote.

[1] Negative values for Sales (due to accounting adjustments), Equity and Book are possible but not likely.

[2] It is from the Fidelity website. If you have no access to it, use Finviz's Rec.: Score =1 if Rec=1 and Score = -1 if Rec = 5.

[3] This metric can be found from many sources. They may use different terms for the same data.

[4] A short squeeze could be coming when a stock is oversold. If the critical problem of the company cannot be recovered easily, change the Score from 1 to -1.

[5] The SPY in the last row is for your information only. SPY is used to measure whether it will beat the market by comparing the return of this stock to the return of the SPY.

[6]   Earnings yield E/P (the reversal of P/E) should be between 8% and 40%.

Score

Score each metric and then sum up all the scores giving you a Grand Score. If the Grand Score is 3 (I use 2 for my passing grade), the stock passes this scoring system. Even if it is a 2, it still deserves further analysis if you have time.

For some reason I do not know why and how to explain this, the top 10% (15% for long term and 5% for short term) of the stocks we score and why they do not perform better than the passing grade. It happens in two of my scoring systems. Be cautious with this as it has happened more than once. The stocks scoring in the bottom 10% are consistently poor performers and that's good. To simplify the usage, ignore the stocks that have scores greater than 7.

The metrics from #1 to #6 are yearly metrics based on the last twelve months except the 'expected P/E'. These are popular value ratios.

Metric 9 and 10 are quarterly comparisons of the same quarter last year. They are readily available from Finviz.com.

Some metrics such as the Analyst's Opinion can be obtained directly from Fidelity. If you do not have access to it, use Rec. from Finviz.com.

Metric

For more information, search the metric in Wikipedia or any financial site.

- P/E.
  Price to Earning is a primary value ratio. The Expected Earning has better predictive power than the one from the last two months.

- Price / Cash Flow (same as Price / Free Cash Flow).
  Cash Flow is one of the few metrics that cannot be manipulated. **It is a red flag when it is increasing fast**. Statistically, it is not a good indicator for the long term but it does add safety.

- Price / Sales.
  Different industries have different averages for this metric. A supermarket business should have a very low ratio. Adjust it according to the industry the stock belongs to.

- Price / Book.
  Usually it is not a good indicator for matured companies such as IBM.

- Equity Summary Score.
  Fidelity has a good handle on this metric. It is based on the past predictive accuracy of the analysts.

- Short Percent (= Shares being shorted / shares outstanding).
  The stock buyers who short the stocks frequently are right more times than they are wrong. The percent between 10% and 20% is high to me.

  However, when it is too high, a short squeeze may be coming. When there are too few shares to sell, the stock price could boost up due to supply and demand. You need to find out the reason why it is so high. If the reason is valid to short the stock, stay away from this stock no matter how high the stock scores. Any scoring system is not sacred and it can be ignored for many situations such as a pending serious lawsuit.

- Insider's Purchase
  When the insiders purchase their company's stock at the market price, most likely the company is doing well. No one knows the company and its sector better than the officials of the company. Ignore options. Ignore the purchases after the insiders sell. Insider Purchases explains why some lowly-scored stocks appreciate fast. Hence, ignore the low scores for stocks with heavy insider purchases and include them for further analysis.

- Profit Margin.
  Ignore or relax this metric during a recession. For those industries that do not have a gross margin, use operating margin instead.

- Revenue growth.
  Ignore or relax this metric during a recession.

- Earning growth.
  Ignore or relax this metric during a recession.

- Intangibles.
  The outlook of the company, its industry and the stock market.

  For simplicity, each outlook scores -1 for poor and 1 for good. Add up the three scores. There is more to it such as serious lawsuits pending, new products, sector rotation, changing market conditions....

  Analyze the high-scored stocks further. If a red flag surfaces, skip the stock. Red flags can be detected from or not from the financial statements. When you use financial statements, ensure they are the most updated ones that usually can be found in the company's website.

Holding Period

The performance monitor uses the holding period of 6 months. After six months, some metrics may change. Hence, evaluate the bought stocks again at that time using the same scoring system. In my last monitor, the metrics did not lose the predictive accuracy, but in the long run it should.

Check out your tax rates for long-term and short-term capital gains. For non-retirement (same as taxable) accounts, you need to make more adjustments such as selling the losers/winners before/after the required holding period for long-term capital loss/gain (as of 2016, it is 366 days to qualify for long-term capital gains).

Fundamentalists are swimming against the tide. It takes time for the market to realize their values. Hence, selling too early (3 months or less) without good reasons is not recommended. When a stock passes the profit target, consider selling it even if it has been bought just over several days ago.

Variations

Enter your changes to this scoring system to suit your investing style and/or different market conditions. The current system uses fundamental metrics. For growth investing, add the appropriate metrics such as PEG, price momentum, etc. This described scoring system **will not work on momentum strategies** (holding stocks less than a month) and day trading.

.

2   Get metric data from Finviz.com

Get data from Finviz.com, a free website. Finviz provides everything on the same screen including the 'Forward (a.k.a. Expected) P/E' that I prefer over P/E.

An Illustration

Use AAPL as an example and note that today is 4/19/13. Enter the value in the last column of the table, and then add the individual scores to get a grand score, which is used to determine whether the stock is value or not.

No.	Metric	Good	Bad	Score	Value
1	P/E (use expected if possible)	Between 2.5 and 12.5, Score = 2	> 50 or < 0, Score = -1	2	7.92
2	Price / Cash Flow[1]	< 12, Score = 1	>30 or < 0, Score = -1	1	8.75
3	Price / Sales[1]	< 0.8, Score = 1	< 0, Score = -1	0	2.2
4	Price / Book	< 1, Score = 1	< 0, Score = -1	0	2.89
5	Equity Summary Score[2]	> 7, Score = 1	< 4, Score = -1	1	
6	Short % (check reason for high %)	Between 30% & 40%, Score = 1[4]	Between 10% & 20%, Score = -1	0	1.12%
7	Insider Purchase[3]	Score = 1		0	Few
8	Gross Margin[3]	> 25%, Score = 1	< 5%, Score = -1	1	42%
	Compare Q to Q last year for #9 to # 10				
9	Revenue Growth[3]	> 15%, Score = 1	< 0, Score = -1	1	18%
10	Earning Growth[3]	> 20%, Score = 1	< 0, Score = -1	-1	-.4%
11	Intangibles	Positive, Score =1	Negative, Score = -1	1	My view
			Grand Score	6	
	AAPL	$390.05	SPY = 155		4/19/2013[5]

Footnote

Step-by-step instructions

1. Bring up Finviz.com from your browser.

2. Enter AAPL for 'Company or Symbol'.

3. The company's profile is described after the metric section. Try Yahoo!Finance if you feel they are not well summarized.

4. The sector is Computer, not one of the sectors (bank, insurer, mine, drug and biotech) we want to be cautious about.

5. It is not a foreign company judging by the address and names of the officers. You need more research on companies that are not well-known.

6. It passes the basic criteria (my recommendations only):

   a. Average Daily Volume higher than 6,000.
   b. Price greater than $2 per share.
   c. Listed in one of the three major exchanges.
   d. Capital Cap greater than 200M.

   Modify, define and / or add your own criteria here. If you want to be in micro-cap stocks or large-cap stocks only, change your criteria accordingly.

7. Enter 1 for Equity Summary Score (used to be Analysts' Opinion) from Fidelity.com. Fidelity uses StarMine which tracks the analysts' past performance. There is a third choice after Finviz: TipRanks and also its consensus on sectors.

8. The Insider Trans (i.e. insider purchases) is positive when the color is green. Scroll down the screen to get the details of the insiders' info. Ignore this metric if the purchases are far below the current price. For more info on Insider Purchase, try out OpenInsider.com.

9. Most other metrics can be retrieved quite easily.

10. The forward (same as expected) P/E is 7.92. Enter 2 for its score (metric #1) as it is within the favorable range. It is also better than the P/E of the last twelve months. It predicts that the earnings would be better in the future.

11. Revenue (same as Sales) Growth compares to the quarter of the prior year to avoid seasonal fluctuations.

12. Earnings Growth has barely passed negative. You decide whether you want to put a 0 or -1 in Score. This metric is more important to Revenue Growth.

13. Add SMA50 (simple moving average for the last 50 sessions) for technical analysis which is not in the original score sheet. If it is over 10%, Score is 1. If it is -10% or less, Score is -1.

14. Determining Intangibles is very subjective. The outlook for Apple and its industry is good, but the current (as of 4/13) market is not.

AAPL scores 6 as of 4/18/13. It passes the passing grade of 3 by 3. It scores one point higher when using Fidelity's Equity Summary Score instead of Finviz's Recom.

Try it yourself. Your score may not be the same as my score as your date of performing this exercise is different from mine.

Some mature companies such as IBM may not score high, but they should be re-considered. Compare its score to its historical scores if it has been scored before. There are always exceptions to any scoring system. There may be current events or situations developing that will not be found in the financial statements such as a new lawsuit or a new, promising drug.

Check out the intangibles, its company's outlook, its industry's outlook and the market's outlook. When the market is plunging, do not buy any stocks with some exceptions such as contra ETFs. Even If the market is risky, you can use the scoring system to have a watch list of stocks ready for when the market returns.

If you trade in shorter terms (less than 3 months), select high-scored stocks and use technical analysis to enter and exit a trade such as SMA-50. It is better to trade stocks that are on their way up.

Again, this scoring system is based on fundamental stocks. The prediction is better on stocks to be held for more than 6 months. Use the scoring system as a guideline. Statistically the scoring system works but there are exceptions otherwise there would be no poor folks. It is better to use a good scoring system to trade stocks than to go without.

Fillers:

For folks who do not want to move to cash during market plunges

If holding cash is boring to you, just throw a gold coin into the ocean every 15 minutes. You will attract a crowd if not a diver or a police man to take you to the nearest mental hospital. In any case, you will make it to the 6 o'clock news.

#Do we need amendments for the Bible

I do not believe in "A tooth for a tooth" but forgiveness.

Screenshot on research screen from Finviz:

AAPL [NASD]
Apple Inc.
Technology | Personal Computers | USA
financial highlights | sta

Index	S&P 500	P/E	10.74	EPS (ttm)	41.89	Insider Own	0.03%	Shs Outstand	938.65M	Perf Week	7.86%
Market Cap	422.37B	Forward P/E	10.16	EPS next Y	44.31	Insider Trans	3.68%	Shs Float	937.18M	Perf Month	5.20%
Income	39.67B	PEG	0.51	EPS next Q	7.40	Inst Own	64.10%	Short Float	2.14%	Perf Quarter	-0.22%
Sales	169.10B	P/S	2.50	EPS this Y	59.51%	Inst Trans	0.00%	Short Ratio	1.17	Perf Half Y	-23.63%
Book/sh	144.12	P/B	3.12	EPS next Y	10.86%	ROA	22.95%	Target Price	543.62	Perf Year	-21.56%
Cash/sh	41.69	P/C	10.79	EPS next 5Y	20.88%	ROE	33.34%	52W Range	385.10 - 697.80	Perf YTD	-14.95%
Dividend	10.60	P/FCF	10.82	EPS past 5Y	62.22%	ROI	28.53%	52W High	-35.51%	Beta	1.00
Dividend %	2.36%	Quick Ratio	1.75	Sales past 5Y	44.81%	Gross Margin	39.50%	52W Low	16.85%	ATR	11.37
Employees	72800	Current Ratio	1.78	Sales Q/Q	11.27%	Oper. Margin	30.92%	RSI (14)	64.29	Volatility	2.29% 2.51%
Optionable	Yes	Debt/Eq	0.00	EPS Q/Q	-17.95%	Profit Margin	23.46%	Rel Volume	0.75	Prev Close	445.52
Shortable	Yes	LT Debt/Eq	0.00	Earnings	Apr 23 AMC	Payout	18.91%	Avg Volume	17.20M	Price	449.98
Recom	2.00	SMA20	7.12%	SMA50	4.01%	SMA200	-16.73%	Volume	12,883,904	Change	1.00%
24-Apr-13	Reiterated		UBS		Buy		$560 → $500				

3   How to use the grand score

This scoring system is used to identify stocks with a higher appreciation potential. Statistically from my last performance monitor, this scoring system works. Sometimes a highly-scored stock may not perform. Check out the intangibles, the company's outlook, its industry's outlook and the market's outlook.

As in any strategy or scoring system, you should use paper trade first and then commit real money gradually and slowly. In any case, do not bet the entire farm on one strategy, and / or one scoring system.

The six steps of trading:

1   Is the market too risky to get in?
2   Screen stocks to reduce the number of stocks to be analyzed.
3   Evaluate stocks using the scoring system in this book.
4   Analyze each stock: Intangible Analysis, Qualitative Analysis and Technical Analysis (skip this one for long-term stocks).
5   Buy the stock.
6   Sell the stock. Analyze and score the purchased stocks to see if they have met your objectives.

All these steps will be described further here:

1. Market risk

If the market is too risky, do not buy any stocks.

2. Screen stocks

There are many good screens (same as searches) available. Try your broker's site first and then Finviz.

3. Score the screened stocks

Screens provide us with a limited number of stocks to evaluate; I prefer less than 10. Reduce the number further using the following criteria if they are not readily available in your screener.

- Take out any foreign companies including those that are listed in the US exchanges if the market does not favor foreign companies. My current performance monitor on this scoring system proves that statistically they are poor performers. Of course, there are exceptions and market conditions could change.

- Take out the following sectors: bank, mining, insurance, drug (generic ok) and biotech. The financial statements do not tell the entire story such as the quality of their loans. You need more help than a scoring system such as subscribing to a newsletter specific to the sector.

- Take out companies with low average volume (less than 8,000 shares for example). You would pay extra for the spread on low-volume stocks.

- It is a personal choice to trade penny stocks that usually have market cap less than 200 M, with prices less than $2, and are not listed in major exchanges. They are risky, but some could provide large price appreciation. There are exceptions. When I traded ALU, I should not have been a penny stock even at $1 per share; its market cap was about 2 B.

4. Analyze each stock

I prefer to analyze stocks that pass the scoring system. The number of stocks to evaluate further depends on how much time available to you. Check out the intangibles. Here are some sources to help you know the company better:

- Yahoo! Finance board. Be careful as there is a lot of bad information too and some are very biased.
- Seeking Alpha. Be warned of the author's hidden agenda. Today there are fewer articles that are free.
- Fidelity's website or your broker's website for research reports.
- Many subscription services such as Value Line and AAII. Check out whether they are available in your local library.
- Zacks for its earnings revision rating and it is free for individual stocks.

5. Buy the stock

Place a buy order close to the market price.

6. Sell the stock

Periodically (about every 6 months) evaluate your purchased stock with the same procedure you buy stocks. If it scores below the passing grade or the market is expected to dip, it could be time to sell.

Afterthoughts

- When not to use any scoring system.
  When you buy at the bottom of a sector or at the bottom of the stock market, all your stocks score low and their outlook would be bad too. When the market recovers, it could be the most profitable time to buy.

- Some stocks with the lowest score surge in a short time. As of 4/25/13, I had TAHO and WLT that had a big surge on the next day after I scored them. I did not know whether it was a dead cat bouncing, or some favorable development or event.

  They usually represent very risky stocks for stocks with lowest scores. When you find these stocks, you either ignore them as suggested by our Adaptive Stock Scoring System, or perform a thorough research. Personally I skip them and have a better sleep.

4   Get metric data from Fidelity

There are many sources to get the same fundamental metrics. This article uses Fidelity and the previous article uses Finviz.com. Other sources are Yahoo!Finance and your broker's website.

An Illustration

Use AAPL as an example and today's date is 4/19/13. Enter the value in the last column of the table and then add the individual scores to get a grand score, which is used to determine whether the stock is value or not.

No.	Metric	Good	Bad	Score	Value
1	P/E (use expected if possible)	Between 2.5 and 12.5, Score = 2	> 50 or < 0, Score =-1	2	8.9
2	Price / Cash Flow	< 12, Score = 1	>30 or < 0, Score = -1	1	8.75
3	Price / Sales[1]	< 0.8, Score = 1	< 0, Score = -1	0	2.2
4	Price / Book	< 1, Score = 1	< 0, Score = -1	0	3.2
5	Analyst's Opinion[2]	> 7, Score = 1	< 4, Score = -1	0	6
6	Short % (check reason for high %)	Between 30% & 40%, Score = 1[4]	Between 10% &20%, Score = -1	0	2%
7	Insider Purchase[3]	Score = 1		0	Few
8	Profit Margin[3]	> 25%, Score = 1	< 5%, Score = -1	1	44%
	#9 to # 10	Compare Q to Q last year			
9	Revenue Growth[3]	> 15%, Score = 1	< 0, Score = -1	1	17.65%
10	Earning Growth[3]	> 20% , Score = 1	< 0, Score = -1	-1	-.4%
11	Intangibles	Positive, Score = 1	Negative, Score= -1	1	My view
			Grand Score	5	
	AAPL 4/19/2013[5]	$390.05	SPY = 155		

Footnote

[1]   If negative values for Sales (due to accounting adjustments), Equity and Book are possible but not likely.

[2]   It is obtained from Fidelity's website.

[3]   This metric can be found from many sources.

[4]   A short squeeze could be coming when a stock is oversold. If a critical problem of the company cannot be recovered easily, change the Score from 1 to -1.

[5]   The last row is for information only. SPY is used to measure whether it will beat the market by comparing the return of this stock to the return of SPY.

Step-by-step instructions

1.   Log on to Fidelity.com.

2.   Select Research and then Stock.

3.   Enter AAPL for 'Company or Symbol'.

4.   The sector is Computer, not one of the sectors (bank, insurer, mine, drug and biotech) which we want to avoid as most metrics do not apply.

5.   It is not a foreign company judging by the address and the names of the officers. Needs more research on those companies that are not well-known.

6.   It passes the basic criteria:
    1   Average Daily Volume is larger than 6,000.
    2   Price is greater than $2 per share.
    3   Belong to one of the three major exchanges.
    4   Market Capitalization is greater than 200M.

    Modify, define and / or add your own criteria here. If you want to be in micro-cap stocks, change your criteria accordingly.

7.   Enter 0 for Equity Summary Score.

8.   Its P/E is 8.9 (not the desired expected P/E). Enter 2 for its score (metric #1) as it is within the favorable range.

9. Click on Detailed Quote. The short interest (on the right side of the screen) is about 2%. Enter 0 for the score for this metric.

10. Click on Key Statistics.

11. Enter the scores for Price /Cash (metric #2), Price / Sales (metric #3) and Price / Book (metric #4).

12. Click on Ownership & Insiders, and then Insider Trends. The trend does not indicate a lot of insider purchases. Enter 0.

13. Revenue Growth (the current quarter compared to the same quarter of last year) is obtained under Growth.

14. Earning Growth (the current quarter compared to the same quarter of last year) is the same as EPS growth (last quarter vs. same quarter prior year) under Growth. It is barely negative, so I treat it as 0%.

15. Determining the intangibles is very subjective. The outlook for Apple and its industry is good, but the current (as of 4/2013) market is risky.

The Grand Score

Sum up all individual scores giving AAPL a grand score of 5. According to my passing grade of 3, AAPL as of 4/18/2013 passes our scoring system by 2.

Try it yourself with the same company or other companies. Your score may not be the same as mine as your date of performing this exercise is different from mine.

Some companies such as IBM may not score high, but they should be re-considered. Compare its score to its historical scores if it has been scored before.

The scoring system is a good guideline only.

I started with IBM instead of AAPL in writing this chapter. It scored two and the day after IBM plunged by 10%. It could be just a coincidence. From my scoring system, IBM is not deeply valued. Its earning is expected to grow and its price had this built-in. When the earnings disappointed, the stock price plunged. That's why I prefer 'Buy Low and Sell High' than 'Buy High and Sell Higher'. Most deeply-valued stocks have nowhere to go but up.

In general, growth companies will not do well in this kind of scoring system, which is based on fundamentals. In this example, AAPL has changed to a value stock from a growth stock.

Check out the intangibles, its company's outlook, its sector's outlook and the market's outlook. If the market is risky, do not buy any stock at all.

If you trade in a shorter term period (less than 3 months), select high-scoring stocks and time the entry and exit via technical analysis. It is better to trade stocks that are on a long-term uptrend. In this case, trend parameters such as SMA-50 are more important than most fundamental metrics.

Again, this scoring system is used to pick up good stocks based on fundamental metrics and hopefully it works most of the time.

Picture Filler:

Screenshot on research screen from Fidelity:

Fidelity.com

Accounts & Trade | News & Insights | Research | Quotes | Guidance & Retirement | Customer Service | Open an Account | Log Out | Investment Products

Research > Stocks >

Saturday, May 4, 2013

Content and data provided by various third parties and Fidelity – Terms of Use

Stock Details

Enter Company or Symbol

AAPL

Key Statistics | Find Symbol | Go

Snapshot
Detailed Quote
Advanced Chart
News & Events
Compare
Analyst Opinions
Research Reports
Key Statistics
Earnings & Dividends
Ownership & Insiders
Financial Statements
Technical Analysis
SEC Filings

OTHER STOCK RESEARCH
Stock Research Overview
Stock Screeners
Explore Research Firms
Watch Lists

DJIA: 14,973.96 +142.38 (0.96%)   NASDAQ: 3,378.63 +38.01 (1.14%)   S&P 500: 1,614.42 +16.83 (1.05%) — Markets closed

Print Format | Help/Glossary | Trading Tutorials

Key Statistics: AAPL

APPLE INC

449.98 ⬆ **4.46 (1.00 %)** AS OF 4:00:00PM ET 05/03/2013

Quotes delayed at least 15 min. Log in for real time quote.

Trade | Add to Watch List | Set Alert | Hypothetical Trade | Option Chain | Price History ▼

Accounting and Governance Risk ⊚

Accounting and Governance Risk (AGR®) is a statistically modeled assessment of corporate integrity which can be used as a confidence level indicator in the company's management and reported financials. Log in for AGR® details.

Valuation

	AAPL	Computers & Peripherals Average	Industry Percentile
Market Cap	$422.37B	$59.53B	100th
P/E (Trailing Twelve Months)	10.74	13.05	64th
P/E (5-Year Average)	16.19	16.99	34th
PEG Ratio (5-Year Projected)	0.51	0.96	46th
Enterprise Value	$418.46B	$282.14B	100th
Price/Cash Flow (Most Recent Quarter)	9.41	10.02	71st
Price/Cash Flow (TTM)	9.44	7.42	69th
Price/Sales (Most Recent Quarter)	2.43	2.93	89th
Price/Sales (TTM)	2.50	2.14	89th
Price/Book	3.43	3.04	82nd

5   Compare the two sources

The following compares the two sources for fundamental metric data: Fidelity and Finviz. You can add your source, if it is not one of the two.

Advantages of Fidelity

- Equity Summary Score.
  I rate it superior. The following are from Fidelity's website.
  "The Equity Summary Score provides a consolidated view of the ratings from a number of independent research providers on Fidelity.com. It uses the providers' relative, historical recommendation performance along with other factors to give you an aggregate, accuracy-weighed indication of the independent research firms' stock sentiment."

- Compare the metrics to the sector.
  There are many metrics such as P/S and Debt / Equity are unique to a specific industry. Super markets should have high sales with low profit margins and some industries such as utilities have high debts. Comparing the company to its peers makes a lot of sense.

- Compare the current P/E to the average P/E for the last five years. It is a sensible way to evaluate its current value. P/E is an important metric but not the sole metric to evaluate a company.

- There are decent reports available free.

Advantages of Finviz

- It is free to everyone while Fidelity allows their customers only to use the website. However, there is no balance required to open an account with Fidelity.

- It saves some time to display most of the metrics on one page.

- Forward P/E. To me, the prediction accuracy is better than the P/E based on the last twelve months.

- Easy to enter Insiders' Purchase.

- Technical analysis indicator is clear.
  I use the 50-day SMA-50%, Simple Moving Average for the last 50 sessions. It is nicely expressed in percentage. I also use Elliot Wave found in Fidelity. The chart displays the trend of the stock clearly.

- The metrics P/C, Current Ratio and Cash /Share are readily available.

Conclusion

Both have their own strengths and weaknesses. Fidelity has been improving their website many times. More often I found more data errors in Finviz and that could be they do not update the database often enough. If you have the time, select the better metrics of the two and find out why if they are different.

Differences in the data from Finviz and Fidelity

On 6/17/2013, I used both systems to score the stock CI. Using Fidelity data, it scored 4 and using Finviz it scored 6. This is why we use the scoring system as a guideline only, and we need to evaluate the stocks further.

Most likely, one's financial data is more updated than the other and / or different evaluations such as Equity Summary Score. Let's check what metrics are identical or very close.

Metric	Finviz	Fidelity
Short %	1%	1%
PEG	1.38	1.38
P/S	0.6	0.6
P/B	2.0	2.1
Earnings growth Q to Q	-84%	-84%
Revenue growth Q to Q	21%	21%
ROE	14%	14%
Total Debt / Equity	52%	53%
Recom. / Equity Summary Score	10	8

The slight difference could be due to the daily fluctuation of the price. Once a while, I found there are big differences.

Filler: Random thoughts

High taxes have been proven bad for the economy and the stock market throughout our history. As Gandhi said, the world has enough resources for all but we're not unselfish enough to share.

6 An extension to the scoring system

The following metrics has not given me good predictive accuracy during this monitoring period. Monitor them in the future. The surprise to me is that ROE did not work this time. I remember a very popular book that just uses ROE as its sole indicator to select stocks. It may be due to too many folks using the same metric.

The following scores are optional. If they are used, add the total to the Grand Score.

No.	Metric	Good	Bad	Score
	Monitor the following			
1	EV / EBITDA			
2	Cash / Market Cap[2]			
3	Technical Analysis[3]	Bull, Score = 1	Bear, Score = -1	
4	ROE[1]	> 35%, Score = 1	< 0, Score = -1	
5	Debt / Equity[1]			
6	Dividend > 3%[4]			
7	PEG			
8	Compare P/E to its average in last 5 years			
9	Compare metrics to their industrial averages			
			Total	
			(Add Total to Grand Score)	

Footnote

1   If the value of Equity is negative, it would affect many related metrics. Price / Cash is easy to find and it is similar to Cash / Market Cap.
2   I use Fidelity's Elliot Wave.
     Finviz.com offers a good alternative. If SMA-50% is more than 10%, it is bullish and if it is less than 10%, it is bearish.
3   The market favors dividend stocks as of 4/13.

My current findings

From my current monitoring I found the following good candidates for future conditions to add to the scoring system:

- The Total Grade and the Cash Flow Grade under Fundamental Grade Blue Chip Growth (not free now). http://navelliergrowth.investorplace.com/bluechip/password/index.php?plocation=%2Fbluechip%2F.
- Zacks (free for individual stocks) grade for short term.
- IBD's composite grade (required a subscription).

The following three should be included for some investors.

- Stocks with dividend yields > 3% and less than 5% (trying to skip the return of capital).
- Debt / Equity.
- Earning growth (current quarter to quarter from the prior year).

Filler: The New Norm

Have you noticed that the index performance was wrong in MarketWatch on 3/1? The Arrow and Color indicated the market was down, but actually it was up. It is so basic. Recently they said the market was down by 2% but actually it was up by 2%.

Before I posted anything in Facebook, they asked me to select all the pictures of a lion. I skipped those pictures with two lions and they told me I was wrong. They need to hire someone who has at least graduated from high school.

#Filler: There is no afterlife according to me

If there is one, the Chinese ghost and the ghost from the west should be the same. Chinese ghosts jump and cannot turn; that's why some bridges are crooked in Chinese gardens. In addition, Chines ghosts stick out their tongues and are quite different from the 'foreign' ghosts. No Chinese see the light from the endo of the tunnel in near-death conditions.

Today's population is about 8 B. From my calculation, the heaven should be very crowded with so many folks going to heaven from Adam's day to today.

7 A scoring system for growth stocks

When the market favors growth stocks more than valued stocks, we would like to change our scoring system to place emphasis on growth.

In the early recovery phase of the market cycle (about one or two years after the market crash), value stocks are favorable. After this period, growth stocks are favorable in general. You can find out which of the following are favorite today: Value or Growth by:

1. Articles from many financial sites.
2. From the performance of an ETF on value stocks (SPYV for example) for the last three months and compare it to an ETF on growth stocks (SPYG for example).
3. From the change of P/E of SPY that simulates the market. If P/E is less than last 3 months, value stocks win. Use PEG (the change of P/E) if you do not keep P/E value in the last 3 months.

When you have a good size of the evaluated stocks for a long time, you can compare their performances and then adjust your scoring system accordingly. The following are the examples of suggested changes for growth stocks.

- Forward E/P. Decrease the number from 2 to 1.
- Earning Growth Q-Q. Increase the number from 1 to 2.
- Sales Growth Q-Q. Increase the number from 1 to 1.5.

8 A scoring system for momentum stocks

When you buy stocks and hold them for a month or less, you do not care about fundamentals but rather the momentum. The momentum metrics such as SMA-20 (Single Moving Average with 20 days average) would be appropriate. The other metrics are: price increases from last 15 and 30 days, earnings revisions and any catalyst (such as a new drug) and insider's purchases.

The rotation by institutional investors is a critical metric for momentum stocks.

Section II: Monitor parameters

Periodically (say half a year), we should monitor the performances of our screens, metrics and our scoring systems and adjust them accordingly. Use the better performing screens more often. Some metrics may lose their predictability due to different market conditions. For example, if value is important in the current market, increase the score value for P/E.

9   Monitor my big gainers

This chapter checks the characteristics of my big winners and the next chapter is on my big losers. The purpose of these two chapters is to demonstrate how to check out the common characteristics of the winners and losers. It also applies to the performances of strategies in the recent market.

Once the common characteristics of our big winners have been identified, search stocks with the screens that perform well. It does not always guarantee the same result. However, it would increase your trading profits more often than not.

In my system of evaluating stocks, it consists of two major parts:

1.   Screen for stocks (same as search).
2.   Analyze the screened stocks (scoring them to start with).

The database
The following data accounts for all the portfolio holdings and the stocks I sold this year in my largest taxable account as of 6/1/2013. My trading strategy keeps track of a lot of stocks, about 50 in this account. This monitor includes 21 stocks (CSCO bought two times), which had a greater than 25% return. The result is too small to draw a concrete conclusion. However, the result of this monitoring is quite compatible with the results of the previous monitors.

To increase your database, consider the following:

- Include the stocks that you have evaluated even if they have not been bought.
- Include the entire year of sold stocks not only YTD.
- Relax your threshold of the big gainers (use 20% instead of 25%).
- Include all accounts. I skip some accounts as they serve different purposes such as one for a momentum strategy.

The results

The results are summarized by the following four tables:

Performance

It should be compared to a market index.

Table 1: Performance Summary.

No. of stocks	Avg. Return	Avg. Annualized	Avg. Holding Period
21	50%	111%	211 days

Source

Table 2: Source of the stocks:

Sources	Web & media	Deeply valued	Acquire candidate	Misc. screens	Short squeeze
No. of stocks	4	3	3	10	1
Annual. Return	75%	53%	204%	115%	164%
Stocks	ADM, BSX, C, EMN	CSCO, CSCO, MSFT	CAMP, FFCH, ADES	ACAT,BIIB CUZ,DGI,NSIT, STRZA,USNA, OMX,DLTR	DECK

The returns are annualized for a better comparison.

Web and Publication.
There are four (from a total of 21) stocks selected from web articles, magazines and newspapers. When I was convinced that there was great appreciation potential, I bought that stock without further evaluation (not recommended). I was lazy but you should do some

evaluation. Need to distinguish whether the authors are pumping-and-dumping the stocks they recommended.

Deeply-valued stocks.
I placed an order with prices about 5% lower than the market prices betting they are still on its way down a little. About three out of six orders were successfully executed. If I have a time machine, I should place market orders on all six as the market is rising. Try to buy all the deeply-valued stocks in the future.

I doubled my normal bet on most of these stocks (CSCO about 4 times). As of 5/2013, these deeply-valued stocks have not realized its potential values and they're the under-performers in the group. However, the average 53% annualized return is nothing to sneeze at!

Update 3/2016. Both CSCO and MSFT have been doing great. From 5/1/2013 to 3/1/2016, their average annualized return is 16% vs SPY's 9%.

Candidates to be acquired.
There are quite a few candidates that would be potentially acquired by other (usually larger) companies in the early recovery of the market cycle (a phase defined by me). However, with plenty of easy money around due to low interest rates and the high corporate cash reserves, it extended the acquisition craze to 2013. This phase will end when the Fed begins to tighten the money supply. This group represents the best return. I should have doubled bet on all of them even though they normally are smaller and unknown companies.

The potential candidates to be acquired are usually smaller companies with a technological edge and/or having a valuable customer base. Sell them when they're no longer candidates.

Miscellaneous screens.
A screen consists of criteria in searching stocks such as P/E < 20. There are 10 stocks from the miscellaneous screens. The performance of each screen is further analyzed. It is better to use the screens that have had better performances recently. My screens are different from yours and some require subscription services, so they will not be disclosed here.

Short squeeze.

The short squeeze happens when the stocks that have been oversold by the shorters. When the stock is oversold, those seeking a short position cannot find the extra shares to be shorted, and sometimes the shorters are forced to cover their shorts due to the high expenses of shorting that stock (interests and dividends).

If the company is not heading towards bankruptcy, any good news would also boost the stock price. This is the typical situation, but it does not work all of the time.

Increase bets on stocks that have better appreciation potential

The confidence in my predictions for CSCO's future is so high that I have bought it four times, and then 2 times for BSX and STRZA. All scored high in my scoring system.

Table 3: Score (using the score system in my book Scoring Stocks:

Avg. Score	Foreign Country	Insider Purchase
3.00	0	1

The average score of 9 stocks is 3 and that is my passing grade in my scoring system. The scoring system is a guideline and we do not have to follow it religiously.

There is not a single foreign stock in this group. I usually do not trust the financial statements of the smaller, foreign countries. The next chapter may convince you to skip most of them at least for now or until it is proven otherwise.

Only one stock has meaningful insiders' purchases out of 21. The database is too small for any conclusion. From my past data, Insiders' Purchases with purchase prices close to the market prices is a good predictor.

By Sectors
Sectors fluctuate in performance.

Table 4: Sectors:

Sector	Tech	Health Care, equip & drug	Consumer goods	Finance	Retail	Misc.
No.	6	4	3	3	2	3
Ann.	77%	230%	102%	60%	57%	78%
Stock	CAMP CSCO, CSCO, DGI, MSFT NSIT	BIIB, BSX, USNA, ADES	ACAT, ADM DECK	C,FFCH, BANR	OMX, DLTR	CUZ, STRZA, EMN

Technology companies.
Technology companies are doing fine, but some are also included in the worst performers described in the next chapter. I rate this sector neutral in this period. Just buy the tech companies with high scores and good outlooks for the company and its sector. In general, tech is doing well in a rising market as consumers have more money for high-tech toys and companies have money to invest such as upgrading their accounting software.

Mining companies.
Miners are not doing so well in this period as described in the next chapter. Monitor this sector as they may be rotated back in when the economy improves with higher demands for industrial ores. There is no miner in the winners' circle.

Health care, medical equipment and drugs.
With the aging population, the companies in health care, drugs (generic preferred), and medical equipment should be doing great. It is the best performing sector.

The last 90-day performances of ETFs specified in sectors are better predictors for sectors.

Conclusion
The database of 50 stocks is too small to make any conclusive conclusion. However, this result is pretty compatible with the previous monitor about 6 months ago that had a large database (about 200 stocks).

Personal performance monitor

There are more sophisticated ways and better tools to monitor performance. Most of them require subscriptions and most are low cost. Some are briefly described together with my experiences.

1. Searches. I have the name of the screens with their average returns. Currently I have about 20 screens I use to search for stocks.

2. Evaluate stocks. Each screened stock should be scored. The performance after 3 months should be compared to the S&P 500 or its corresponding index such as using QQQ for tech stocks. The prediction for the accuracy of each fundamental metric should also be checked periodically.

In addition, I divide the database into short term (3 to 6 months) and long term (about 12 months).

Afterthoughts

- Health care sector. Click here for a SA article. (http://seekingalpha.com/article/1503232-bull-of-the-day-biogen)

- We need to check how the portfolio performs when the market goes down. The best performance is when it beats the market in both market directions. However, there is no evergreen strategy. You should use a strategy that is supposed to be favorable in specific market conditions.

Links

Selling short:
http://en.wikipedia.org/wiki/Sell_short

Short squeeze:
http://en.wikipedia.org/wiki/Short_squeeze

Oversold:
http://www.investopedia.com/terms/o/oversold.asp

10   Monitor my big losses

This article is a repeat of the last one except with my big losers. It is more important to learn from big losers, so we will reduce buying losers that fit into a certain pattern.

The database

The database is smaller due to the current rising market. Partly, it is due to my avoiding the potentia4l losers from previous monitors.

I delete the stocks which have less than a 25% loss. It only has 11 stocks from a total of about 50. A database of 11 stocks is too small to draw any conclusions. However, the results are compatible with my previous results. In other words, they follow similar patterns.

The results

As in the last chapter, the results are summarized by the following four tables:

Table 1: Performance Summary.

No. of stocks	Avg. Return	Avg. Annualized	Avg. Holding period
11	-43%	-163%	223 days

From here on, annualized returns will be used.

Table 2: Source of the stocks:

Sources	Deeply valued	Acquire candidates	Misc. screens	Short squeezed
No.	0	0	11	0
Annualized Return			-163%	
Stocks			BPI,NTE, SIGA,SIM, VELT,STEC, IAG, END,DEER, CRUS,HXM	

All the stocks here were from my screens. I find the screens with better recent performances perform better than the average; it means the selection of the screens work.

There is not a single stock from the categories from web & publication, deeply-valued list, being acquired or being short squeezed that we find in the last chapter.

Table 3: Score (using the score system):

Avg. Score	Foreign Country
1.86	6
Annualized	-216%

The average score is 1.86 (3 is a passing grade defined in my book Scoring Stocks). Four (out of 11) stocks have not been scored. If I scored them, I may not buy them. My mistake was not scoring them.

There is not a single stock with a meaningful insider purchase. I have encountered that the lowly-scored stocks with meaningful insider purchases appreciate more than the average. Most foreign companies do not have to list insider information.

There are too many foreign stocks in this loser group while there is not a single foreign stock among the best performers. If I skipped these six stocks, I would have saved a bundle. We cannot go back in time, but it is a strong guide for the future. I do not know why I still bought foreign stocks as they did not perform well in the last monitoring period.

Luckily I did not place any double bets on any of these losers.

Table 4: Sectors:

Sector	Tech	Miner	Health care, equip and drug	Misc.
No.	4	3	1	2
Annual. Return	-128%	-131%	-34%	-734%
Stocks	NTE,VELT, STEC,CRUS	SIM,IAG END	SIGA	BPI,HXM

Miners are not doing well in this period. Watch out for this sector as it flows with the global economy. Most miners are foreign companies. I do not trust their financial data except from Canada and Australia.

Technology companies are not doing so well. However, we have some technology companies included as the top performers as described in the last article. The only difference is most of the losers are smaller companies and most are foreign companies. I rate Tech a neutral. Buy those tech companies with high scores, headquartered in the U.S. and good outlooks.

Performance

The combined annualized return of my big losers is 73%. It is smaller due to no double bets on losers.

Update I did another performance analysis in 1/2015 including all the stocks that had been screened but I had not bought. Except one from 25 stocks, the losers are either lowly scored, foreign companies and/or miners. Nine stocks had a grade of F from Blue Chip Growth (not free any more). Surprisingly six of them had heavy insider purchases.

Conclusion

The database of 11 stocks is too small to draw a conclusion. However, the conclusion of this monitoring is very similar to the one I did with the larger database of about 200 stocks 6 months ago.

In combining the results of the two chapters, my conclusions are:

1. The stocks with high scores perform better than those with low scores in my two monitors.

2. Screens (searches) are monitored separately with about a total of 200 stocks and from about 20 screens. Buying candidates that are acquisition prospects have been profitable for this year and 2003.

3. From this monitor and the previous, foreign companies including those companies listed in the U.S. exchanges have been underperforming compared to the U.S. stocks.

4. Miners do not perform this time. It could be due to the so-called sector rotation. When the economy improves or this sector is recognized as being oversold, most industrial metals would return to the former price levels.

5. The better performances from sector health care, medical equipment, or drugs are responding to the aging population.

6. My previous monitors had identified that foreign companies did not perform on the average. I still have several foreign companies this time. If I had omitted them, the return of this portfolio would be far better. I need to follow my recent results.

7. I bet less on the risky companies (most were small companies and /or had low scores) and bet more on better companies.

8. Read articles on this topic. Here is one.

#Filler: An interview of a successful fund manager

This is a typical interview of fund managers that I read in magazines. Learn from what are applicable to us and ignore most ideas that do not make sense. Let me argue for and against them. The name is withdrawn to protect the innocent.

1. "Never can predict market crashes". Look at my simple chart that has successfully detected the two crashes since 2000.

2. "No. 1 in the last 10 years, but lags the market in the last 5 years". The last five years is more important to his investors. It could also be due to his assets having grown more than 15 times. Another bad sign for his future performance.

3. "Seldom sell". Most stocks change a lot in 3 years. Portfolio churning improves the quality of a portfolio. I prefer the one that turns over in a year.

4. "Visiting many companies". It is not applicable to our retail investors. I also hear many stories that the officers set up a good show to fool the analysts. We can look at the financial sheets that cannot lie easily and legally for a long period of time.

5. "Water is a long-term trend". Yes, it is. However, I had a bad experience using this idea too early.

6. He continued to show how some of his stocks made over 100%. Let me remind you that he did not beat the market in the last five years. Hence, he was not being kind enough to show his losers, which may be more important than learning from his winners.

11   My performance monitor

This article serves as an illustration on how to do your own monitor. Most data are from 7/2015. By the time you read this article, the findings could be outdated. Hence, learn how to monitor performances from this article. In addition, it is based on my stocks actually screened and the number of stocks is too limited to draw a general conclusion.

There are two monitors, one for short term and one for long term. Score 3 is my passing score for both short term and long term.

The score results:

Score =	Avg.	< 3	3	4	5	6	7	>=8
Short	7%	2%	8%	11%	7%	14%	11%	-10%
Long	8%	4%	13%	14%	7%	21%	4%	-10%

Explanation

- The score system works if the higher the score, the better the performance. It is to some extent with the exceptions of Score 7, 7 and >=8.
- From the table, I should use 3 as the passing grade for both short term and long term.
- Do not buy stocks when the score is 8 or higher. It is consistent from my previous monitors. I do not know why. I assume that when the stock is too good to be true, most likely it is not.
- When the stock scores between 3 and 7 inclusively, it is a buy. It is quite similar to the previous monitors. It also destroys the price efficiency theory.

How reliable is the score

As stated, it only applies to me for this test period. The reliability also depends on the size of the sample. The following shows the number of stocks.

	Total	< 3	3	4	5	6	7	>8
Short	747	397	113	97	69	41	27	3
Long	555	299	75	70	53	30	25	3

How fundamental metrics score

The following table shows us the predictability of the metrics.

Short Term: (7% return for the average)

Metric	Parm. 1	No.	%	Parm. 2	No.	%	Predict.
EY	>14	203	4%	<5	94	0%	Good
Blue Chip BC	A	150	7%	F	63	-4%	Good
BC Funda-mentals	A	191	14%	F	66	-11%	Good
Fidelity Analyst	Buy	150	10%	Sell	279	3%	Good
P/B	<1	162	1%	>2	333	9%	Bad
ROE	>25	180	9%	<2	110	4%	Good
GRT	<20	71	-4%	>25	685	6%	Good
P/CF	<20	179	8%	>30	99	5%	Good
Earn Gr Q-Q	>50%	227	6%	< 5%	68	0%	Good
Sales Gr Q-Q	>25%	153	7%	<5%	154	0%	Good
Debt/E	<.1	172	15%	>1.5	69	2%	Good
RSI(14)	>60	85	9%	<40	33	-2%	Good
SMA 200%	>5	94	1%	<-5	19	-4%	Good

Long Term: (8% return for the average)

Metric	Parm. 1	No.	%	Parm. 2	No.	%	Predict.
EY	>20	28	3%	<5	77	-1%	Good
Blue Chip	A	99	8%	F	62	-4%	Good
Blue Chip Fund.	A	178	15%	F	65	- 11%	Good
Fidelity Analyst	Buy	90	17%	Sell	208	4%	Good
P/B	<1	15	2%	>2	227	9%	Bad
ROE	>25	135	11%	<2	93	4%	Good
GRT	<20	67	-3%	>25	488	9%	Good
P/CF	<20	133	11%	>30	54	9%	Good
Earn Gro Q-Q	>50%	141	11%	< 5%	68	0%	Good
Sales Gro Q-Q	>25%	97	8%	<5%	110	2%	Good
Debt/E	<.1	168	15%	>1.5	61	4%	Good

RSI(14)	>60	27	22%		<40	7	0%	Bad

Explanation

- I skip the metrics from various subscription services I subscribed.
- The returns are used for comparison only ignoring many standard yardsticks such as comparing it to the market index, and excluding dividends.
- P/B is not a good metric from my samples. RSI(14) is fine for the short term but not useful for the long term. However, due to the limited data on RSI(14), they are not conclusive. SMA-200% is not available for the long term as it is a new one for me.
- Short term is usually about 4 months and long term is about 12 months on the average; this is just a general guideline.
- Some data are both long term and short term by playing some tricks by not updating the stock prices of some data; some data could be eligible for both short term and long term as they are close in the specified ranges.
- The predication of the metric is good if they're as expected.
- Your score is derived from the above metrics. Weigh more on the metrics with better predictability. Modify your scoring system based on your monitor.
- EY (E/P) is expected (a.k.a. forward) earnings yield. GRT is earning growth rate.
- The stock has a higher chance of appreciation if it is rated A in both the Blue Chip composite score and its fundamental score, Buy in Fidelity's Equity Summary Score, ROE> 25%, GRT > 25%, Debt/Equity < 10% and Earnings Growth > 50% for the long term. It is quite similar to the short term which should include SMA-50.

When you cannot find any stocks, relax the selection. I would start with Earnings Growth > 30% as my primary metric.

Filler: Smart male pigs

Chinese use 'pig' as an adjective to describe stupidity such as pig brain. Pigs are smart enough to convince many religions not to eat them. If you're in the old-fashion farm, you can see all the female pigs line up every afternoon to mate with the male pig. I bet you want to be a male pig in your next life. I must have a pig brain to say so. LOL.

12   Metric performances & market cycle

From my limited testing on the last two market cycles (2000 and 2008), some metrics perform better than others. This is for reference only. I select the following metrics. Grades are estimates from a hypothetical vendor.

- EY, Expected Earning Yield (Expected Earnings/Price).
- TG, Timing Grade. It is based on price momentum, increases in sales and profits...
- VG, Value Grade. It is based on fundamentals such as P/E, Debt/Equity...

Cycle stages	Performers	Bad Performers
Year before plunge	TG, EY	VG
Plunge to bottom	TG	EY
Early Recovery	EY, VG	
Up and Peak	EY, TG	
All stages	EY, TG, VG	

- They are in descending order. For example in All Stages, EY has better performance than TG.
- EY and TG are good in almost all phases. The exception for EP is poor performance during market plunges. Aggressive users can short the stocks that have high EY at this stage.
- EY and increasing EY turn out to be a best performer during Early Recovery, a phase in the market cycle defined by me. In this phase buy stocks with high EY and VG. It has been proven in 2003 and 2009.
- I expect EY is part of the VG. However, my tests tell me otherwise.
- EY, TG and VG are metrics close to the status of 'evergreen'.
- I also have other metrics that may not be relevant to the general discussion. They are growth of earnings, growth of E/P and growth of dividend.
- The performances of many AAII strategic screens are provided. Separate them in the phases of a market cycle and make the conclusions accordingly.
- To check performance of metrics, I use Google Finance to create a portfolio and download the current prices to a spreadsheet.

13   Investing: Long Term vs. Short Term

I claim short-term investing is not gambling. Short-term investing can make you good money, if you have the correct knowledge and discipline in this strategy. Actually I use both a long-term strategy and a short-term strategy and monitor the performances. I would invest more on the strategy that is more profitable among the two in the current market. In general, I use taxable accounts for long term investing.

Long-term investing
Fundamentals are important. Technical Analysis may be used to time the entry and exit. Everyone has their own favorite fundamentals. Here are mine:

1. EV/EBITDA is a good way to measure the value of a company. This metric has its advantages and disadvantages over P/E. It is better as it includes cash (including short-term securities), and debts. I have seen a small company having more cash than the total market cap and total liabilities. If there is no major liabilities such as pending lawsuits, the buy decision is a no-brainer. The only disadvantage is most of them used earnings of the last twelve months, not the forward (same as expected) earnings.

   EBITDA/EV (EVEBITDA flipped over) is easier to understand and it takes care of the negative earnings if available. To illustrate, if it is 35%, you can receive your entire investment in about 3 years.

2. The next important metric is free cash flow. The company can have a lot of sales and good reported earnings, but the cash flow is poor. You have to find out the reason why. If their vendors are not paying, most likely it is a serious account payable problem; 2000 is a common problem to many companies.

3. As described in this book, many free websites evaluate the stock for you such as Fidelity's Equity Summary Score.

   Most analysts are good in estimating earnings but due to the conflict of interest, they may not publish reports for the public.

4. Let the profit rise. I usually sell my stocks when they double. I have missed many profits. I recommend using trailing stops for these rocket stocks.

5. You're swimming against the tide with value stocks. Be patient as it takes time for the market to recognize its true value. Review the purchased stocks routinely to ensure there is no major problem.

"Buy and hold" should be replaced by "Buy and monitor. Many big companies have gone bankrupt or close to such as GM and U.S. Steel. Polaroid and Kodak suffered by advance of digital cameras. Many retailers suffer from the rise of Amazon.com. The pandemic of 2020 will make some sectors poorer such as travel industries.

Short-term investing
In general, it is opposite of long-term investing. Some metrics have more weights in scoring them. Price momentum is more important than fundamentals. To illustrate, the discovery of a new drug will not be shown in their fundamentals, but the rise in the stock price will. Everyone has their own favorite technical metrics. Here are mine that can be found from Finviz.com:

1. SMA, Single Moving Average.
    It indicates the uptrend when it is positive. SMA20 is for short term (20-days average) and SMA50 for intermediate term.

2. RSI(14). When it is over 65, the stock may be overbought. Hence, the chance of reversing from the uptrend is high.

3. There are many technical patterns. Experience is important to check whether they are useful to you. I usually select both Daily and Weekly for Time Frames in Finviz.com. Personally I prefer "Double Top" for down trend and "Double Bottom" for uptrend.

4. Daily Volume is the confirmation.

As opposite of Long-Term Investing, the holding period is relatively short. Mine is one or two months. I also have mental stops in case the trend is reversed. The uptrend may be reversed when the SMA and/or RSI(14) decrease.

Section III: Simple techniques

For starters, just trade ETFs such as SPY (an ETF simulating the market) and you can skip the latter chapters in evaluating stocks. In essence, you only spend a few minutes to time the market.

If you have less than $50,000 to invest, just buy ETFs. Improve your investing skills by reading investment articles from this book, talk to your broker/financial adviser and/or subscribe to AAII. When your portfolio grows to $50,000, invest about $300 annually on a subscription such as GuruFocus, Value Line, IBD or Zacks.

For the long term, knowledge is most important in your investing life. Retail investors have a lot of advantages over fund managers. However, I advise you not to be a trader and most beginner day traders lose money. Hence, you should ignore the fabulous trade systems that claim to be. Statistically most amateur traders lose money as they cannot compete with experienced, disciplined traders. Start with paper trading which is usually available from your broker.

1   Simplest market timing

Why market timing

Before 2000, market timing was a waste of time. However after that, we have had two market plunges with the average loss of about 45%. It sounds harder to time the market than it actually is. We have a simple technique to detect market plunges and when to reenter the market. Our objective is reducing the loss to 25%.

Market timing depends on charts; the following describes how to use chart information without creating charts. Most charts will not identify the peaks and bottoms of the market as they depend on data (i.e. the stock prices). However, it would reduce further losses. It is simpler than it sounds. Just follow the procedure below.

The first part of this technique detects market plunges, and the second part advises you when to reenter the market. It applies to individual stocks too. It also works to detect the trend of a sector (entering an ETF for the specific sector instead of SPY) and a specific stock.

How to detect market plunges without charts (a.k.a. Death Cross)
1. Bring up Finviz.com.

2. Enter SPY (or any ETF that simulates the market) or RSP for equally weighed SPY.

3. If SMA-200% is positive, it indicates that the market plunge has not been detected and you can skip the following steps.

4. The market is plunging if SMA-50% is more negative than SMA-200%. To illustrate this condition, SMA-200% is -2% and SMA-50% is -5%.

5. Sell most stocks starting with the riskiest ones first such as the ones with negative earnings, high P/Es and/or high Debt/Equity. Obtain this info from Finviz.com by entering the symbol of the stock you own.

6. Conservative investors should sell only those overpriced stocks. Aggressive investors should sell all stocks. Extremely aggressive investors should sell all stocks, buy contra ETFs, and even short stocks. I do not recommend beginners to be aggressive.

When to return to the market (a.k.a. Golden Cross)

Use the above in a reversed sense to detect whether the market has been recovering. However, when the SMA-200% turns positive, I would start buying value stocks (low P/E but the 'E' has to be positive, and/or low Debt/Equity).

1. Bring up Finviz.com.

2. Enter SPY (or any ETF that simulates the market).

3. If SMA-200% is negative, the market is not recovering, and you can skip the following steps.

4. Sell all contra ETFs and close all shorts if you have any.

5. Market recovery is confirmed when SMA-50% is more positive than SMA-200%. To illustrate this condition, SMA-200% is 2% and SMA-50% is 5%. Commit a large percent of cash (or all cash for aggressive

investors) to stocks. If you do not know what to buy, buy SPY or an ETF that simulates the market.

How often to check the market timing indicators

Do the above once a month. When the SPY price is closer to SMA actions percentage, perform the above once a week. The charts and data for market timing described in this book are based on SMA-350 (Simple Moving Average) that is more preferable than this simple procedure, but it requires some simple charting.

Nothing is perfect

If the market timing is perfect, there would be no poor folks. The major 'defects' are:

- It does not detect the peak / bottom as it depends on past data. However, it would save you a lot during the crash.
- It is hard to determine whether it is a correction or a crash.
- From 2000 to 2010, there was only one false signal. The indicator tells you to exit and then tells you to reenter the market shortly. In most cases, you do not lose a lot. After 2010, we have more false signals.
- The market may not be rational or may be influenced due to specific conditions such as excessive printing of USD. If you do not mind charting, use SMA 350 (or 400) using SPY. Buy when the price is above SMA-350 (or SMA-400), and sell otherwise. SMA-400 reduces the number of false signals, but it is not nimble.

2   Simplest way to evaluate stocks

Beginners should trade ETFs only. This chapter is for the readers who are ready or getting ready to trade stocks. In general, ETFs are diversified, less volatile than trading stocks. However, stocks offer higher profit but higher risk.

Many stock researches have already been done recently and some are available free of charge. I have no affiliation with Fidelity except I retired from it. You can open an account with them with no balance. Their Equity Summary Score is one of the best indicators; I check out **value** stocks with scores higher than 8. Concentrate on fundamental metrics such as P/E for long-term holds, and momentum metrics for short-term holds. Add criteria to limit the number of screened stocks. Finviz.com is a free screener.

Several sources

The popular ones are Morningstar, Value Line, The Street and Zacks (currently free for rankings of individual stocks). If they are not free, check out whether they are available from your local library. I have 3 simple ways to evaluate stocks starting with the simplest. In addition, read the articles on the selected stocks from Fidelity, Finviz, Seeking Alpha and many other sources for further evaluation.

Fidelity

Select only stocks that have Fidelity's Equity Summary Score 8 or higher. There is tons of information about a stock. Once in a while I did not agree with this score such as SHOP and ZM that scored high in August, 2020. Include the following for your analysis.

A modified stock selection based on a magazine article

Most metrics are available from Finviz except EV/EBITDA.

1. Forward P/E (expected earnings and not based on the last twelve months). It should range from 5 to 15 (10 to 25 for high tech stocks). EV/EBITDA (from Yahoo!Finance) is a better choice as it includes the debts and cash than P/E; it would be more effective if it uses forward earnings. If you do not use EV/EBITDA,

ensure Debt/Equity is less than 0.5 except for the debt-intensive industries.

2. ROE (Return of Equity) measures how well the company uses the capital. I prefer stocks with ROE greater than 5%.

3. Volatility. Conservative investors should select stocks with a beta of less than one (i.e. less volatile).

4. Insider Transactions for sales (i.e. negative) should be less than 5%. If it is -5%, most likely the insiders are dumping it.

5. Compare the metrics such as P/E and Debt/Equity to its five-year average and its competitors (available in Fidelity).

6. Momentum. Check out the SMA-50 (actually SMA-50%) and SMA-200. Ideally they should be positive. SMA-50% is especially important for stocks you do not want to keep for a long time.

7. Check out articles on the stock as some recent events (for example a new lawsuit) have not been included in the metrics.

8. Compare the trend of the sector this stock is in. Under Finviz, enter the related sector ETF.

Summary
The sources are Fidelity (Equity Summary Score and various comparisons), Finviz and Yahoo!Finance (for EV/EBITDA). Value stocks should be held longer.

Category	Score / Metric	Value /Momentum
Score	Fidelity's Equity Summary Score	Both
Value	EV/EBITDA	Value
	P/E cheaper compared to 5-year avg.	Value
	P/E cheaper compared to its sector.	Value
	Insider Purchases	Both
Safety	Debt/Equity	Value

	Compare it to its sector.	Value
Momentum	50-SMA%	Momentum
	200-SMA% (for long term holds).	Value
Articles	Check out latest events	Both
Market	No purchase if market is risky.	Momentum

A simple scoring system using Finviz
Bring up Finviz.com and then enter the stock symbol.

No.	Metric	Good	Bad	Score
1	Forward P/E[1]	Between 2.5 and 12.5, Score = 2	> 50 or < 0, Score = -1	
2	P/ FCF[1]	< 12, Score = 1	>30 or < 0, Score = -1	
3	P/S[1]	< 0.8, Score = 1	< 0, Score = -1	
4	P/ B[1]	< 1, Score = 1	< 0, Score = -1	
	Compare quarter to quarter of last year			
5	Sales Q/Q	> 15%, Score = 1	< 0, Score = -1	
6	EPS Q/Q	> 20% , Score = 1	< 0, Score = -1	
			Grand Score	
	Stock Symbol Date[2]	Current Price	SPY	

Footnote
[1]   Negative values for Sales (due to accounting adjustments), Equity and Book are possible but not likely.
[2]   The last row is for your information only. SPY is used to measure whether it will beat the market by comparing the return of this stock to the return of SPY.

The Score
Score each metric and sum up all the scores giving the Grand Score. If the Grand Score is 3, the stock passes this scoring system. Even if it is a 2, it still deserves further analysis if you have time. You may want to add scores from other vendors. To illustrate on using

Fidelity, add 1 to the score if Fidelity's Equity Summary score is 8 or higher. Monitor the performance after every 6 months or so to see whether this scoring system beats the market.

Very basic advice for beginners

Beginners should stick with U.S. stocks with Market Cap greater than 800 M (million), Debt/Equity less than .25 (25%) except for debt-intensive industries such as utilities and airlines and Forward P/E between 5 to 20 (25 for high-tech companies). These metrics are all available from Finviz.com, which is free.

Do not have more than 20% of your portfolio in one stock (unless it is an ETF or mutual fund) and do not have more than 30% of your portfolio in one sector.

For more conservative investors, buy non-volatile stocks whose beta (available from Yahoo!Finance) is less than 1. Beta of 1 represents the market (the S&P 500 index). For example, a stock with beta 1.5 statistically fluctuates more than 50% of the market and hence it is very volatile.

Try paper trading to check out your strategy and your skill in trading stocks. If your broker does not provide one, use a spreadsheet to record your trades or check the availability of simulator.investopedia.com.

#Filler: Silence is golden

I am glad I did not give advice to a friend who had to decide whether to take a lump sum payment or an annuity. The correction in March, 2020 would wipe out a lot of his portfolio if he took the lump sum payment. No one would share his profits when the predictions are correct, but the blame if it does not materialize.

It is the same in investing that nothing is certain. With educated guesses, we should have more rights than wrongs especially in the long run.

3   Simplest technical analysis

When the stock, the sector that the stock is in and the market are all above its SMA-N averages (Single Moving Average for the last N sessions), most likely the stock is trending up.

1. Bring up Finviz.com from your browser.

2. Enter SPY. Write down the SMA-200 (Single Moving Average for 200 sessions). Positive numbers indicate that the trend for the market is up.

   However, the market could be peaking or overbought. Be careful when SMA-200 is over 5% and / or RSI(14) is over 65%. RSI is a metric on over bought / under bought.

3. Enter the sector ETF the stock is in. Write down the SMA-50. Positive numbers indicate that trend for the sector is up.

   However, the sector could be peaking or overbought. Be careful when the SMA-200 is over 10% and / or RSI(14) is over 65%.

4. Enter the stock symbol. If your average holding period of the stocks is 200, use SMA-200 and so on. I recommend SMA-200 for holding value stocks long term and SMA-50 for momentum stocks. Write down the SMA-N for your stock. Positive numbers indicate that the trend is up.

   However, the stock could be peaking or overbought. Be careful when the SMA-200 (or SMA-50) is over 25% and / or RSI(14) is over 65%.

If the above three criteria and the fundamental criteria are satisfied, most likely it is a good buy. If you buy sector ETFs or mutual funds only, you can skip step #4. In any case, use stop loss to protect your investment.

#Filler: The Ten Commandments of Investing.
http://www.investopedia.com/articles/basics/07/10commandments.asp

- Set goals. * Personal finances in order. * Ask questions. * Do not follow the herd. * Due diligence. * Be humble. * Be patient. * Be moderate. * No

Section IV: Finding stocks

The worst way to find stocks is via TV. Many analysts have hidden agenda. More than one time, a fund manager or an analyst recommended a stock while his company was unloading it. Many have conflicting interests. Some may buy the stock before they recommend it. Unless you have reliable insider information (be warned that it is illegal to use insider information), trust your own research.

1 Where the web sites are

- **Free and simple screen sites**

  They are described in this article or type the following
  http://stocks.about.com/od/researchtools/a/071909screenlist.htm

  - Yahoo!Finance.
    Click here or type
    http://screener.finance.yahoo.com/stocks.html

  - Finviz.
    Click here or type
    http://Finviz.com/screener.ashx

    How to scan using Finviz (YouTube).
    https://www.YouTube.com/watch?v=aQ_0FTg9Cfw

    Screening using technical indicators (particularly useful for momentum stocks).
    https://www.YouTube.com/watch?v=RZRP2NeSX0s

  - Your broker.
    Fidelity's screens are more sophisticated than most.

  - More options: Google, CNBC.com and Moringstar.com.

  Here is a list.
  http://stocks.about.com/od/researchtools/a/071909screenlist.htm

- **Sophisticated screens (usually not free)**

  Most of them are more complicated and need time to learn. Both Vector Vest and Stock123 provide historical databases for back testing your screens. Zacks has an earnings revision database at extra cost. GuruFocus has an easy-to-use but powerful screen function.

  AAII provides screened stocks from various screens in its low-priced subscription. Both AAII and Value Line take care of some specific industries, but they provide no historical database at least for regular subscriptions. AAII provides historical performance summaries of their screens included in its subscription.

Afterthoughts

Here are the links to screens provided by Marketwatch and NASDAQ.
http://www.marketwatch.com/tools/stockre...
http://www.nasdaq.com/reference/stock-sc...

How to find quality stocks.
http://seekingalpha.com/article/2381395-how-to-identify-quality-stocks-and-is-there-really-alpha-to-be-had

Filler
"Sell in May" could be a self-fulfilled prophecy. I prefer to sell on April 1 and come back on Oct. 15 to avoid the herd.

2 A simple tutorial

From your browser, bring up Yahoo!Finance's screener by clicking here or type http://screener.finance.yahoo.com/stocks.html.

Select the following to select stocks with share price > $5, market cap > 250 mil, P/E < 15, Est. Earning Growths up to 20% for 1 year and up to 5% for 5 years, and Buy Rating = 1.

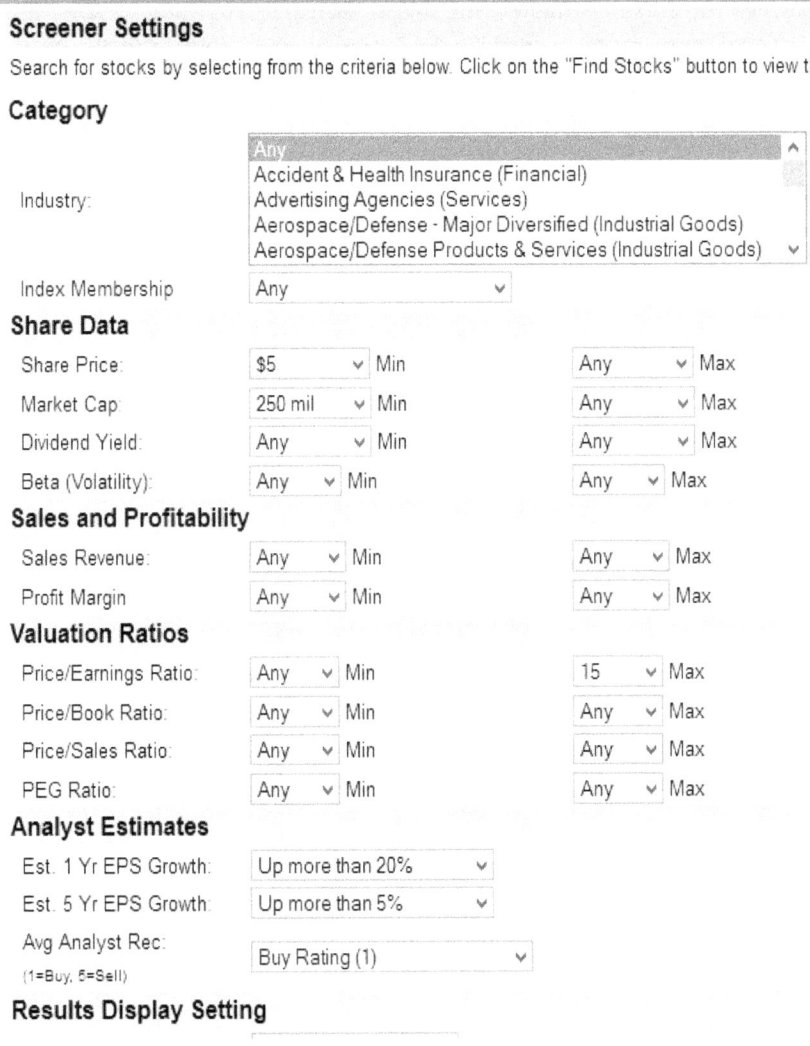

Screener Settings

Search for stocks by selecting from the criteria below. Click on the "Find Stocks" button to view th

Category

Industry:	Any
	Accident & Health Insurance (Financial)
	Advertising Agencies (Services)
	Aerospace/Defense - Major Diversified (Industrial Goods)
	Aerospace/Defense Products & Services (Industrial Goods)

Index Membership   Any

Share Data

Share Price:	$5	Min	Any	Max
Market Cap:	250 mil	Min	Any	Max
Dividend Yield:	Any	Min	Any	Max
Beta (Volatility):	Any	Min	Any	Max

Sales and Profitability

| Sales Revenue: | Any | Min | Any | Max |
| Profit Margin | Any | Min | Any | Max |

Valuation Ratios

Price/Earnings Ratio:	Any	Min	15	Max
Price/Book Ratio:	Any	Min	Any	Max
Price/Sales Ratio:	Any	Min	Any	Max
PEG Ratio:	Any	Min	Any	Max

Analyst Estimates

Est. 1 Yr EPS Growth:	Up more than 20%
Est. 5 Yr EPS Growth:	Up more than 5%
Avg Analyst Rec: (1=Buy, 5=Sell)	Buy Rating (1)

Results Display Setting

Click on Find Stocks.

As of 9/21/2013, you cannot find any stocks based on these criteria. Relax the filter by taking out the Est. 1-Yr Growth and the 5-Yr Growth. Click on Find Stocks again. You should find several stocks.

The stocks with '.xx' at the end could be the stocks you may not want to consider. They could be foreign stocks in foreign exchanges, listed in pink sheets, etc. That's why most screens allow you to select Exchanges.

One common problem with this screen is that it may not handle negative or zero earning. So, you may want to select stocks whose earnings are greater than zero.

Tips

- Predictions are just predictions, so do not follow the predictors blindly even those (myself included) with good records.

- No one including all the Federal Reserve chairmen and all the Nobel-Prize winners in economics can predict market plunges.

- Bubbles have existed throughout our history. Bubbles occur due to the excessive valuation initially driven up by the big institutional investors.

---

3   Fidelity

Fidelity offers a strong screen function. The most unique feature is incorporating its Equity Summary Score (used to be Analyst's Opinion) and some outside researches such as Zacks and Ford.

From the main menu, select "News and Research", "Screen and Filter" and then "Start a screen".

The following example selects stocks with the following criteria: Security Price (2 to 250), Market Cap. (300 and above), Equity Summary Score (8 and above), Zacks (Strongest) and Ford (Strongest).

It displays the 10 stocks. Research each stock. Read the News about each stock. You may want to use Finviz.com, Yahoo!Finance and other sources to double check.

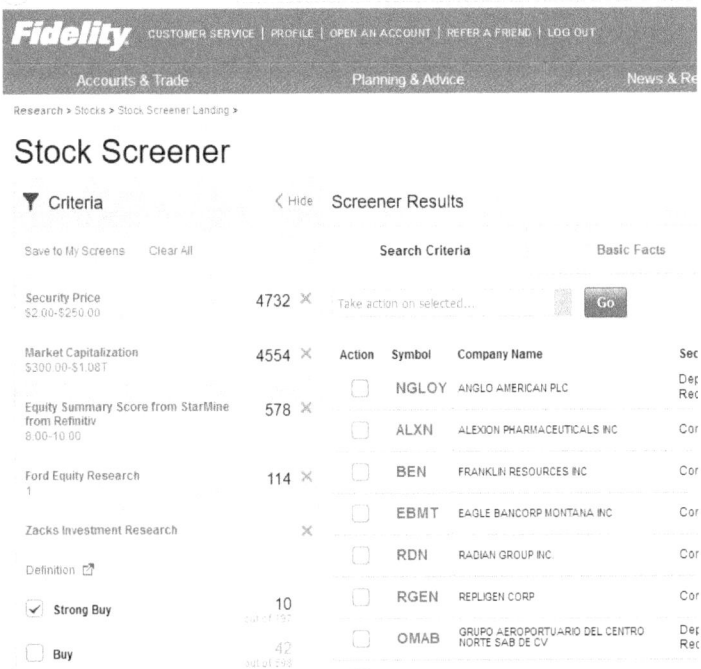

The following describes some of the features.

- Equity Summary Score. It is one of the major metrics I use in my proprietary scoring systems. They are not available to many small stocks. From my limited database in 7/2015 and for short durations, the results are:

Short Term: (7% return for the average)

Metric	Parm. 1	No. of Stocks	%		Parm. 2	No.	%	Predictability
Fidelity Analyst	Buy	150	10%		Sell	279	3%	Good

Long Term: (8% return for the average)

Metric	Parm. 1	No. of Stocks	%		Parm. 2	No.	%	Predictability
Fidelity Analyst	Buy	90	17%		Sell	208	4%	Good

It has its own limits, but they are very minor to me.

First, it does not have a historical database for verifying the screen performance such as the return after a year. However, I do not know any site that provides this function free. To work around this, I save the results in a spread sheet and update the performance.

Secondly, it does not provide many other filter criteria that can be found in other systems such as technical indicators or insider transactions found in Finviz.com. I use other sites for further evaluation.

Most investors should find that this screening is a very good tool and very easy to use.

4   NASDAQ

It is quite similar to GuruFocus's screens in some aspects, but quite simplified. Currently it is free. Bring up Nasqaq.com from your browser. Select "Investing" and then "Guru Screeners".

The following is an illustration on 6/9/2016. Select "P/E Growth Investors" and change "Some" to "Strong". Click on "Go".

I had 5 stocks with "Strong": THO, MPX, GGAL (ADR), BRDCY (ADR) and BMA (ADR). If you prefer U.S. companies only, you only have THO and MPX and both had a desirable "Proj. P/E" under 20.

Alternatively to reduce the number of screened stocks, include stocks with "Some Strong". Sort the "Proj. P/E" in ascending order. If it is blank, most likely it is losing money or there is no estimate for this stock. Use Finviz.com or Yahoo!Finance to confirm.

PEG (P/E growth) is a growth metric and it is available for sorting. You need to evaluate each screened stock. For example, a low P/E stock may not be good if it has excessive debt, or serious pending lawsuits.

Click on the stock THO. It explains how Peter and other gurus score this stock. If you use 70% as a passing grade, 7 gurus rate it a pass and 3 gurus rated it failed.

Click on "Detailed Analysis". Peter rates 4 "Pass" and 2 "Neutral" together with the description.

Try other gurus and select the guru(s) who fit your requirements. For example, if you are a value investor, find a guru or gurus using value metrics.

5   *Finviz.com screener*

You should use fundamental metrics for fundamental stocks, growth metrics for growth stocks, momentum metrics for momentum stocks, or a combination. Basically you want to keep the fundamental stocks longer so the market would realize their values.

Finviz.com provides a screening function incorporating both fundamental and technical metrics and is one of the best free sites. Bring up Finviz.com in your browser and select screener. You have 4 tabs: Descriptive, Fundamental, Technical and All. It has the following features:

- The criteria specified can be saved but the number is limited.
- The searched stocks can be saved in a portfolio (for paper trading and performance monitoring).
- Technical indicators.
- For an extra fee, you can have a historical database. This would help you to test your strategies. The historical database is quite limited for some technical parameters only.
- Some advanced technical indicators work well especially useful in momentum trading.
- Use technical patterns. My favorites are Head and Shoulder and Double Bottoms (Peaks).
- Combine fundamental metrics and technical metrics to narrow down your selection.
- Combine fundamental metrics and technical metrics to narrow down your selection.
- Add Insider Trans (> 5% for me), Short Squeeze (> 20%), etc. for specific purposes.
- Candlesticks is hard to master. You need to read a book dedicated to it.

http://www.investopedia.com/terms/c/candlestick.asp
https://www.youtube.com/watch?v=FsqoV1aVrUc&list=WL&index=56

Finviz's screener lacks the following features:

- Stocks with prices trending up in the last several weeks (such as increasing X% in the previous week).

- Using exponential moving averages that supposedly have better predictive power than simple moving averages for momentum investing.
- Selecting ranges such as selecting all three major exchanges and market cap ranges.
- P/E for an ETF. It can be obtained from other sources such as ETFdb.com.
- When the earnings (E) is negative, you may have the wrong values for P/E and the metrics using E. For example, if you want stocks with P/E less than 20, the screener returns you stocks with negative earnings.
- Combine fundamental metrics and technical metrics to narrow down your selection.

All of these missing features can be worked around. The paid version may provide better functions.

Links:

Investopedia.
http://www.investopedia.com/university/features-of-Finviz-elite/other-chart-features.asp

How to scan using Finviz (YouTube).
https://www.YouTube.com/watch?v=aQ_0FTg9Cfw
https://www.youtube.com/watch?v=tHtovnCY6uY&list=WL&index=96 (Recommended)

Finviz's screener tutorial.
https://www.youtube.com/watch?v=glMtwB7OVf4&list=WL&index=56

Swing trading
https://www.youtube.com/watch?v=M8sNMhPJINU&list=WL&index=55

Screening using technical indicators (YouTube).
https://www.YouTube.com/watch?v=RZRP2NeSXOs

A screener example

The following is an example. Fine tune the selection criteria according to your personal criteria and risk tolerance.

- Bring up Finviz.com from your browser. Select Screener, the third tab. As of 3/24/2015, we have 7066 stocks.

- For illustration purposes, we would like to find stocks with double bottoms, a positive technical indicator. Select the Technical tab. Select Pattern and then Double Bottom. Now we have 257 stocks.

- Select the Fundamental tab that is next to the Technical tab. Select Forward P/E and then select "under 20". Now, we have 86 stocks.

- Select Debt/Equity less than .5. Now, we have 45 stocks. Some industries such as utilities are traditionally high in debt, so you can use 'less than 1'.

- Select EPS growth Q-to-Q over 10%. Now, we have 19 stocks.

- Select the Description tab. Select Country to USA. Now, we have 17 stocks.

- Select Price > 1. Select Avg. Volume "Over 100K". Select Float Short "Under 10%. Select Analyst Recs. "Buy or better". Now we have 9 stocks.

  Now we can evaluate them one by one using Fundamental Analysis, Intangible Analysis, Qualitative Analysis and Technical Analysis. The purpose of screening is to filter the 7000 stocks to a small number (9 stocks in this case).

Skip the stocks that have the Earnings Date within 2 weeks. If you already have too many stocks in the same industry, skip that stock. You can save the screen when you have registered with Finviz.com. It is free. Check the performance of your selections after 3 months or so.
Other sources

Paper trade and check the actual performance before investing your money. Many popular screens provided by many sites worked before but may not work now. It could be too many folks using the same strategy. Hence it is important to check the current performances of the screen you are using. For yardstick, use SPY or similar ETF that simulates the market. Here are some sources beside Finviz.com.

Your broker

Most broker sites have screen functions. Some have screens to simulate what a specific guru such as what Warren Buffett would buy.

IBD (a subscription service)

From my check on the IBD 50, they're good in the last 10 years, but not that good in the last 5 years – the victim of their own success? They provide stocks from their screens. Most screens are for momentum stocks and large caps. Here are the updated days for specific lists as of this writing.

Stocks Group	Published
Sector Leaders	Daily
Stock spotlight	Daily
Top World	Daily
IBD 50	Mon. and Wed.
Weekly Review	Fri.
Big Cap 20	Tue.

You may want to check out individual stocks with Stock Checkup and then analyze them again. The following are good parameters: Composite Rating, Industry Ranking (finer and better than Sector Ranking) and Relative Price. Understand their parameters and apply accordingly - the same for most other vendors.

IBD prefers large and growing companies with institutional ownership. Some of their parameters may not make sense for small, value and/or turn around companies.

Common parameters

Different styles of investing use different parameters for screening stocks. Here is my suggested parameters in using Finviz.com. Vary them to your risk tolerance and market conditions. Finviz.com is not complete in all functions, but it could the best free screener that incorporates both the fundamental and the technical criteria. The first table is for Value and the next one for Growth. The last one is for finding stocks that the institutional investors are trading.

Screening value stocks

Value Screens	Common	Penny	Micro Cap	Dividend
General				
Market Cap (M)	>500 M	<50 M	50 -200 M	+Mid(>2B)
Price	>5	< 5	1-15	>5
In all 3 Exchanges	In	Not In	Most are In	In
Avg. Volume	>100K	>5K	>10K	>100K
Country	USA	USA	USA	USA
Dividend%				>3%
Float Short	<10%	<10%	<10%	<10%
Analyst Rec	Buy or +	Buy or + if avail.	Buy or +	Buy or +
Fundamental				
Forward P/E	<20	<20	<20	<25
ROE	>10	>10	>5	>15
QQ earning	>0			>0
QQ sales	>0			>0
PEG	<1	<1	<1	<1.2
Payout%				20-50%
P/S	<10	<10	<10	<10
Technical				
Price above 200 SMA	Yes	Yes	Yes	Yes
RSI(14)	< 70	< 70	< 70	< 70

There may be no analysts or very few following penny stocks and micro-cap stocks. QQ is quarter to quarter.

Screening Growth Stocks

Growth Screen	Common	Technical	Momentum
General			
Market Cap (M)	>50	> 1,000	>500
Price	>1	>10	>5
Exchanges (Major 3)	In	In	In
Avg. Volume	>50K	>200K	>100K
Fundamental			
Forward P/E	<30	<30	<30
Return of Equity	>5	>0	>0
QQ earning	>10%	>15%	>20%
QQ sales	>5%	> 5%	>10%
PEG	<1	<1	<1
Analyst recs.	Buy or +		
Technical			
Price above 200 SMA	Yes	Yes	
50 SMA	Yes	Yes	Yes
RSI	< 75	< 75	

Short-term trends are important for momentum stocks.

Explanation

The above are suggestions only. Adjust them to your personal preferences and risk tolerance.

- Finviz screener lacks ranges, such as market cap and multiple of exchanges. Most Finviz's parameters do not have a range option such as Exchanges, so you need to run the screen three times, one for each of the three major exchanges.

- Average Volume. When the price of the stock is less than $3, double the average volume requirement. In most cases, 10K is quite acceptable to me. When the volume is small, you may have to pay more (a.k.a. spread) to trade.

- There are many fundamental metrics such as Debt/Equity and Price/Free Cash Flow that are not included here, but they should be included in your further evaluation. Each industry sector has different thresholds. For example, the P/S is very different for a supermarket rather than a high-tech company. Compare the company to the average value of the companies in the same sector. Many sites including GuruFocus.com and Fidelity.com have the average values displayed.

- For momentum stock, you can ignore most of the fundamentals and concentrate on the price trend such as SMA-20% (Simple Moving Average for the last 20 trade sessions) and SMA-50%. The higher the percent, the higher it is away from its own average. You do not want to hold momentum stocks too long (max. 3 months unless the momentum is still uptrend); personally my max. is 1 month.

- For growth stocks, ensure the PEG (P/E growth), quarter-to-quarter earnings and quarter-to-quarter sales are above the averages in its own sector and/or the market.

- Technical analysis favors large cap stocks with large volumes. I prefer stocks with positive earnings and they are fundamentally sound.

- When the SMA-20%, SMA-50% and SMA-200% are all positive, they should be in an uptrend.

- RSI(14) indicates whether the stock is oversold (>65) or under bought (<30). The range is my suggestion only.

- You may want to check out your strategies using a virtual account from your broker.

A general guideline for Institutional investors

Criteria	Value
Description	
Relative Volume	Over 2 M
Country	USA usually
Institution Ownership	Over 50%
Technical	
SMA-200	>10%
Volatility	Week – Over 3%
RSI(14)	>40%

Fundamental	
Market Cap	>1B
ROE	>10%

- Again, these are my suggested metrics. I prefer USA companies and many are global companies. If you use foreign countries, ensure they are larger companies and/or in countries that have regulations similar to our SEC's.
- For value investors, select Forward P/E less than 20 (25 for high-tech companies) and their Earnings are positive.
- Check out how many analysts are following the stocks that you are interested in.

To illustrate, I find 12 stocks. I narrow them down to 3. First, I skip all stocks that already have had more than 10% rise recently. They may have risen too high already.

Select profitable stocks with forward P/E less than 25. "Debt/Equity" is less than .5 (50%). Then, ROI is higher than 25%. Stop when you have reached the optimal number of stocks (3 for me in this example).

If you find too many stocks, tighten the criteria and vice versa. Save the criteria and the selected stocks in a portfolio for paper trading.

Filler: Irresponsible is my best defense

I told my date that I would not be responsible after the second drink due to the lack of an enzyme.

Filler
Starbucks is being sued for too many ice cubes in the ice coffee. If he wins, he would sue MacDonald's, Burger King... and be a billionaire. Why did I not think of this? The lady won for the spilling of hot coffee. The jury did not know that eventually we had to pay for all of these and made the lawyers rich. Too many unproductive lawyers makes it tough to operate a business including small businesses. In many countries besides the U.S., the one who sues and loses has to pay for court expenses.

6   Sectors to be cautious with

There are many reasons to be very cautious when investing in the following sectors. However, Technical Analysis (a.k.a. charting) would give you more hints than the fundamentals for stocks for these sectors. If the big guys are dumping, most likely Technical Analysis (or the simplest SMA-20) would tell you that.

Loan companies/banks

The financial statements do not show the quality of their loan portfolios. Following this advice, you may be able to skip the banks that melted down in 2007. The peak of Citigroup is $550 and several banks went bankrupt.

Many metrics are not relevant for banks such as Debt/Equity and EBIT. The rising interest rate would be good for banks' profits.

Drug (generic is ok)

Understanding the complexities of the drug pipelines, its potential profits for new drugs and the expiration of the current drugs may not worth the effort for most retail investors. In addition, a serious lawsuit and / or a serious problem with a drug could wipe out a good percentage of the stock price. When a drug shows unpromising sign(s) in any trial phase, the stock could plunge and vice versa.

Miners

It is extremely difficult to estimate how much ore (sometimes a miner owns several different types of ores and/or of different grades in the same or different mines) that a company has. It is further complicated by the complexities to extract and transport them. When the total of these costs is greater than its production price, the company will not be profitable. Understanding the market for ore futures is another discipline.

Many mining companies are in foreign countries such as Canada, Australia and countries in South America. Their financial statements of Canada and Australia are more trustworthy than most other emerging countries.

One potential problem of mining companies from many emerging countries is nationalization.

Mining rare earth ore is extremely risky when the profit depends on how China, a major producer of these ores, will price these ores. After China announced the export restrictions on rare earth elements, several non-Chinese companies announced to reopen their mines for rare earths, but few have made any profits as of 2013. Developed countries have stricter environmental regulations.

Coal and eventually oil suffer from the rising use of cleaner energy such as solar and wind.

Insurance companies
Insurance companies profit by:

1. The difference between the total premiums received and the total claims minus expenses in running the company.

2. How well they invest the premiums; you pay your premiums earlier than you may collect from any claims.

They can protect the profits in #1 by restricting claims by natural disasters such as earthquakes and by re-insuring. However, a bad disaster could wipe out a lot of their profits.

Even if the insurance company shows you its investment portfolio, most of us, the retail investors, do not have the time and expertise to analyze it.

Emerging countries (not a sector)
Their financial statements especially from small companies cannot be trusted, and many countries use different accounting standards. Emerging countries are where the economic growth is. I trade FXI, an ETF, rather than individual Chinese companies. I have lost a lot in small Chinese companies due to frauds and politics. To check out whether the stock is an ADR, try ADR.COM (https://www.adr.com/).

Stocks with low volumes (not a sector)
Most likely you pay a high spread to trade these stocks. They can be manipulated easier. I had a hard time trying to sell a stock owned by a few owners.

For simplicity, I trade stocks with the average daily trade volume over 6,000 shares (double it if the price is $2 or less). A better way could be by calculating the percent of your trade quantity / average daily trade volume; it would reduce the effect of penny stocks that have larger volumes due to the low prices.

Good business and bad business

Banking is a good business in a growing economy. My deposit in them makes virtually zero interest, and they loan the same money making 3%. If they are more cautious in loaning, they should make good profits.

Restaurant is an easy business to run, but it is very hard to make good money. With the rising of minimal wages, it will get even tougher. That could be the reason for so many coupons today. The high-end restaurants are doing better due to the rising stock market. The pandemic of 2020 would wipe out a lot of small restaurants.

Retailing is a tough business. Look at the top 10 retailers 15 years ago, I can only find two including Macy's that are still surviving. Most are either went bankrupt or being acquired. Even Macy's was not in good financial shape. Amazon is the killer.

Airlines are a tough business. You can tell by the average increase in fares in the last 10 years. It cannot even beat inflation. They have to charge you for everything. The next frontier charge is the rest room (especially for long-distance flights). Now I understand why they call themselves "Frontier Air". As of 2014, it is quite profitable due to mergers and lower fuel cost. The pandemic of 2020 may be the toughest time for airlines. As of 5/2020, Boeing has many serious troubles and they can only survive with a bailout from the government.

There are several software companies that produce software such as the virus detecting programs and tax preparation software. The customers faithfully buy new versions every year. That's great business.

7   Performance of my screens

I monitor the performance of my top screens every 6 months or so. Here is my September, 2013 summary. The purpose is identifying the screens that have performed well recently. It is for illustration purpose only. All returns are annualized. They are sorted by Grand Avg. in descending order.

Screen	Last Monitor 2/13	Current Test Avg.	Long-term Avg.	Short-term Avg.	Grand Avg.	Avail.
EP	39%	66%			59%	75%
BB3	35%	70%			53%	25%
LPSER	-21%	72%			49%	75%
MN	19%	53%			45%	75%
CW	64%	49%	39%	20%	38%	100%
LR	30%	37%			35%	100%
TT	30%	26%	71%	8%	35%	100%
TV2	50%	76%	14%	19%	35%	100%
BFSCB	5%	38%			31%	100%
DO	29%	24%	30%		28%	100%
AR	56%	53%	23%	6%	28%	100%
BE	81%	44%	10%	13%	25%	100%
FA	16%	27%			25%	100%
BS5BV	21%	25%			24%	100%
SE		53%	20%	-3%	23%	100%
CAO	-3%	17%	37%	12%	21%	100%
...	...	...	---	...	...	
Avg.	34%	19%	23%	5%	19%	

Screen.
They are the abbreviations. To illustrate, CAO is the screen looking for candidates for acquisition with low market caps. I have about 25 production screens. They have been selected among over 100 screens.

Last Monitor 2/2013.
Copied from the "Current Test Avg." from my last monitor in 2/2013.

Current Test Avg.

It is the average of the four tests on recent months. The four test dates are: 03/11/13 to 7/9/13, 4/9/13 to 8/7/13, 5/9/13 to 8/17/13 and 6/8/13 to 9/6/13. They are about 4 months apart. It is the most important average to reflect what worked recently.

Long-term Avg.
It is the long-term performance (about 12 months) of the actual, screened stocks. These are stocks that have been actually screened and some may have been purchased.

Short-term Avg.
It is the short-term performance (about 6 months) of the actual, screened stocks.

Grand Avg.
It is a weighted average of the above 4 return categories (Last Monitor, Current Test Avg., Long-Term Avg. and Short-Term Avg.) and they're sorted in descending order.

Run the top screens first as they have given me better returns in the past. It does not guarantee that they will perform as well as before, but they have a better chance to perform well than the screens scored below the average.

Availability.
To illustrate, if the screen found stocks in 1 out of the 4 tests, it is 25% available. These screens may not have enough data for prediction on the future results and there is a higher chance that I will not find any stocks using these screens.

Observations
The following are the personal findings on my own screens. You can do something similar to separate your top screens from the rest of your screens. Test and monitor the performances of your own screens.

- Usually the top half of the screens from the last monitor show up in this monitor though their ranks may vary.

- CAO in the last monitor should be better than it indicates. At least two companies had been acquired and they had very good returns. These two companies did not show up in the test as they're taken out from the historical database; it is termed as survivorship bias.

- CW is quite consistent to the last monitor.

- EP and BB3 have not found any stocks in actual usage. MN proves to be a good screen in these two performance monitors. I missed the opportunities to make good money from this screen – my mistake.

- LPSER is a risky screen demonstrated here and from the previous monitors. I prefer not to take unnecessary risk. Include a column of maximum drawdown as it is a good indicator to avoid risky screens.

- LR was below the average and that's why it had not been used. It is above the average in this monitor, so it will be used to some small extent.

- TT is above the average in these two monitors. The returns of screened stocks during this monitor are better in both long term and short term and hence it will be used.

- The original table (not shown here) has comparisons to SPY (an ETF simulating the market). Beating the market is my yardstick. If most of your screens beat the market, most likely they will beat the market again. However, there are exceptions such as when the market is plunging. In this case, value stocks are better than growth stocks, and cash is the king.

  The market during my last monitor is better than this period. If the return of SPY is negative in the last three months, there is a good chance that the market is trending down.

- There are some screens that just do not perform for a long while. They will not even be monitored next time. However, when the phase of the market cycle changes, the performance of these screens may respond differently.

- The test results are not always consistent. It could be due to my limited data, or the market does not behave normally.

Section V: Fundamental metrics

1   Fundamental metrics

ROE

Return of equity (ROE = Net Income / Equity) could be the most important financial indicator to determine how well the management is doing their job. However, in recent years, this metric has been overused and loses its prediction reliability.

The company's return on equity for at least the last five years would indicate how the stock price endures major financial downturns as well as upturns.

Comparing the ROE to the average ROE for the sector is a good indicator on how well the company is managed compared to its peers. Some sectors including utilities have low average ROEs.

Market Cap (Capitalization)

Market Cap = Total no. of outstanding shares * share price

I recommend the beginners buy U.S. stocks with a market cap greater than 800 M (million). Here are the current conventions (everyone's convention is different) and they should be adjusted to inflation.

Class	Market Cap (million)
Nano Cap	< $50M
Micro Cap	$50M to $250M
Small Cap	$250M to $1B (billion)
Mid Cap	$1B to $10B
Large Cap (Blue Chip)	$10B to $50B
Mega Cap	>50B

The higher the cap is, usually the less risky the stock would be. Nano Cap and Micro Cap are reserved for speculators or owners of the companies. Small Cap and Mid Cap are for knowledgeable investors as most institutional investors would skip these stocks in these caps especially Small Cap. Large Cap, Mega Cap and some Mid Cap are the stocks traded by institutional investors. They are thoroughly researched continuously.

My metrics

My current favorites are Forward P/E, PEG, Fidelity's Equity Summary Score, Short % of outstanding shares, Free Cash Flow, ROE and Debt Load / Equity.

In addition, I use many summarized metrics from different sources. For example, one of my subscription services gives me a composite rank for fundamentals and another one for momentum.   To illustrate, click here for Blue Chip Growth which is no longer free for stock analysis. Enter IBM as the stock symbol. As of 2/2013, it gives C for a Total Grade, D for Quantity Grade and B for Fundamental Grade. The Total Grade is usually a composite grade of other grades.

Use the metrics to screen through the stocks to reduce the number of stocks for further consideration.

Mid, high and low values of common metrics

Metric	Mid Range	Low Range	High Range
P/E (last 12 months)	< 10	>40	< 4
Price / Cash Flow	< 12	>30	< 4
Price / Sales	< 2.5	>3	< .2
Price / Book	< 2.0	>4	< .2
PEG	< 1.5	>2	< .2

High Range means good values (although in this table it means low numbers), but sometimes it is too good to be true. Low Range means bad values. To illustrate, many internet stocks in 2000 had P/E over 40 (bad) while a neglected bargain stock has a P/E of 3 (supposed to be good). A bargain could also mean they could have some hidden problems. In reality, I prefer the Mid Range. Using P/E to illustrate, it should be between 4 and 10. Adjust the range according to your personal tolerance and the current market conditions. If the market trend is up, you may want to relax the range to 5 to 12 for example otherwise you cannot find too many stocks for further evaluation.

These values are my selections based on data for about 10 years. They are used for predicting the performance of a stock in a year; review the ranges every 6 months in the current market.

The metrics with the high-range and mid-range values offer better predictions for the stock price appreciation. From the above table, the stocks with the low-range values have a better chance than other stocks to lose money in a year or so. Some favorable numbers could be high values instead of low values such as ROE.

However, the range values could change. When the market favors momentum or you do not keep stocks for less than a month or so, the momentum metrics including PEG and price growth could be better predictors. We need to check to see whether the current market favors which metrics: Value or Growth – some websites and subscription services identify the current favorite. In addition, the performance of each metric should be evaluated every 3 to 6 months. In addition, new range values need to be adjusted with the above table.

Fundamental metrics take a longer time (about 6-12 months vs. 1 month for momentum metrics) for the performance to materialize. The metrics in the above table besides PEG are all fundamental metrics. Except for financial stocks, P/B is always worthless.

Examples of searching with high range values

Stocks with low-range values for most metrics (such as 40 in P/E in the above table) could be risky. Hence, select the stocks with the mid-range value (e.g. 10 for P/E). Avoid the low-range values indicated by the metrics.

Here is one example of selecting stocks with high range values of P/E and P/B. Most likely, you will not find too many stocks with these criteria.

$$E > 0 \quad \text{and}$$
$$P/E < 4 \text{ and}$$
$$P/B < .2$$

E is earning per share and we need the company to be profitable.

High range values could indicate something is wrong with the company, e.g. a lawsuit pending. I would consider a P/E of less than 4 is suspicious. However, very small companies are often neglected by the market, so they could be solid companies. Don't forget to do your due diligence and spend more time in thoroughly evaluating the stock and its industry.

The stocks with the low-range values have a greater chance of losing money in the next year or so. That is proven statistically as a group despite some exceptions. AMZN[2] is not a valued stock by its high P/E or its high P/B. However, if the company is investing for the future by building infrastructure and capturing the market share, you may ignore these unfavorable metrics. Personally I prefer fundamentally sound companies today.

Note. P/B is not a good metric for established companies and / or companies with a lot of research such as IBM. Many metric formulae are outdated due to ignoring intellectual properties, patents and market appeals such as brand names.

Example of a search for mid-range values

E > 0 and
P/E < 10 and
P/E > 4

In this case, you only include companies with positive earnings and P/Es within the range from 4 to 10 exclusively. You should find many companies with the mid-range values of P/Es.

Add other filters such as minimum price, market cap and average volume. If you do not find too many stocks, relax your criteria (start with mid-range values in the table), and vice versa to limit the number of stocks. If you usually find stocks with a screen but not today, it usually means that the market is overvalued and that you cannot find many bargain stocks.

Again, it is the first step to narrow down the number of stocks to be analyzed. Your metrics will not cover stocks with special situations. For example, IBM always has had a high Price/Book value for as long as I can remember and therefore it does not mean it should be excluded.

The searches based on fundamental metrics help us to narrow stocks for further evaluation. Occasionally I abandon the scoring system for some stocks under special conditions.

Compare a company's metrics to its sector's averages
This could be the most powerful comparison: Compare Apples to Apples.

You may want to compare the metrics of a company to the averages of that sector. The average of supermarket's P/S is extremely low and hence it has no meaning to compare a supermarket's P/S to most other sectors. Some sectors like utilities need high debt to run a utility company.

However, when the average P/E or other metric of a sector is suddenly lower than its historical average, it could mean that sector is out-of-favor and/or the sector is having a better value.

This following table compares Apple to its sector and a retail sector on a specific date for illustration. All the metrics will change.

Metric	Apple	Computer	Retail
P/E	11	19	24
(5 year average)	16	17	15
PEG	.6	N/A	1.4
Price /Cash Flow	9.4	8.1	9.2
Price /Book	3.3	3.0	3.6
EPS Growth	-6%	-42%	2.6%
(last 5 years)	62%	45%	11%
Operating Margin	20%	15%	8%
ROE	30%	14%	19%
Debt / Equity	2%	7%	88%
Inventory Turnover	76%	53%	4.55x

From the above table, some metrics only make sense for an industrial sector (Computer for Apple). In this case, you may want to compare AAPL to Computer, and not to Retail.

"Debt / Equity" indicates that the retail sector needs to borrow more than the computer sector for example. Of course retail stores has high Inventory Turnover.

Top down approach

First, compare whether the market is risky. Second, select the best sector; there are many sites including Finviz.com to select the best sector. Then compare the fundamental metrics of the major stocks within that sector.

Some metrics do not apply

Using financial institutions as an example, usually P/B is more useful than P/CF. However, the quality of a loan (not a metric here) is more important than all metrics as we found out in 2007. P/S is more important for retails. However, the expected P/E is most important for most other sectors.

When you believe a sector is the currently best (a criterion available in many screeners), select the best stocks in this sector.

Compare metrics to its five-year average

If the company's five-year average of P/E (available from Fidelity and many other sites) is 20 and today it is 10. It is 100% under-valued by this standard. Also, you may want to try other metrics such as debt/equity and compare it to the five-year average.

Growth Metrics

The growth metrics are growth rates of the stock price, sales, earnings, etc. They are useful for growth investors.

Even for value investors, the earnings growth rate is very important, as most stocks with substantial gains have increased their earnings growth first. If the earnings has grown but the price remains the same (i.e. PEG), then the potential for price appreciation will be higher and most likely it will return to the historical average P/E.

Momentum Metrics

Momentum metrics is part of growth. The rates of increase of the stock price, the volume... are the major metrics. Earnings revision is another one especially in earnings announcement seasons (usually 4 times a year).

Fidelity and many subscription services provide a composite rank with name Timely or similar name. The following could be part of this Timely score: SMA-50, Q-Q sales increase and recent price appreciation. In my momentum portfolio, I use these metrics and ignore all the other metrics as my average holding period is less than 30 days for momentum strategies.

Insiders' buying

Insiders sell their stocks for many reasons. When insiders buy a lot of their companies' stocks at market prices, take notice. Insiders know better than anyone about the health of their companies and their industries.

Select Insiders' purchases from one of the available sites such as Finviz.com. Ignore the option exercises. I prefer the high ratios of Net Total Purchase Value / Market Cap and the purchases by more than one insider. Be careful that the insiders purchase the stocks after selling a similar amount of stock in a brief time span.

OpenInsider is a good site for this info.
InsiderSights is a good one too with more capable tools that would take more time to learn.

Where to get the metrics
You can get this information from the website with no or low cost such as Finviz.com, your broker's site, AAII (very low cost) and Fidelity.

The following subscriptions are at a little higher cost but they are still less than $1,000 per year: Value Line, IBD, Zacks, VectorVest and Stock Screen 123. Many data from different vendors are duplicated such as P/E. You will save time by concentrating on one or two sources.

Many vendors provide a composite metric such as a value metric to cover P/E, debt... and a timing metric to cover Technical Analysis indicators, PEG, price appreciation rate...

Short % is a useful metric available in Finviz.com. For Fidelity customers, you can click on Research and then Stock. Enter the stock name, and then click on Detailed. I find Fidelity's Analysts' Opinions quite useful.

Finviz.com provides a lot of useful information free of charge. It also provides a screen function. The 'Help' button describes Finviz's functions and all the metrics monitored.

Other sources are: Insider Cow, NASDAQ Guru Analysis ...

Monitor the recent performance of the metrics
The predictability of most metrics has proven not to perform consistently as many investors and fund managers found out. My theory is that the specific metric works better in some market conditions than others. To test which ones work better currently, check their performance in the last three months and use those that perform well. This is what my scoring system in the book Scoring Stocks is based on.

Why some metrics fail sometimes
Most investors are using metrics to screen stocks, but few are successful consistently. Some investment companies have top analysts dedicated to projects looking for the right strategy. My guesses why they fail are:

1. Metrics need to be monitored to see its effectiveness on current market conditions.

2. Besides fundamental metrics, there are many intangibles.

3. When they have too many followers on the same metrics, they will not work such as ROE in the last several years.

4. Fundamentals need time (at least 6 months) to reflect the value of the stock. You're swimming against the tide as a fundamentalist. Trading momentum stocks using basic fundamentals will not work.

5. Watch out 'Garbage in and garbage out'. Some emerging countries do not have an organization similar to SEC to ensure the integrity of the financial statements of a company and some audit firms are being paid to cover their eyes. Even though there are frauds in some U.S. companies and with their auditors.

6. The metrics may be derived from obsolete financial statements. Check out the date. The most updated one could be available from the company's website.

7. Some companies borrow a lot of money to dress up the metrics such as P/E and ROE. They will look good short-term but not long-term. Ensure the debt/equity has not been increased recently for this purpose. I recall one utility spin-off had incredible fundamentals except the debt load. It is so high that all these fundamentals will deteriorate in the future due to servicing its high debts.

Footnote

[1] The stocks are classified into sector and then sectors are divided into industries (same as sub sectors). For example, oil is a sector and oil exploration and oil services are industries under the oil sector. For simplicity, I intermix the terms here as many sectors do not need further sub classifications for this discussion.

[2] AMZN is not a value stock by any standard. As of 1/1/2013, its P/E (from last 12 months) is 157 and P/B is 15. Both fall far into my low-range values. Its price rises from 256 from 1/1/13 to 270 today (1/22/13). Today its P/E is ridiculously over 3,000. The investors are betting AMZN's internet sales will take over the concrete stores and its investors do not care about profit but rather for market share. Does it sound familiar in the internet era? Its price momentum is indicated positively by any chart. It may be a good stock for traders, but it is too risky for a swing trader and a long-term investor like me (yes, I wear two hats). I do not short stocks in a rising market, but this could be an exception.

Afterthoughts

- The only recommendation from a very popular investment book I read is to select stocks by the return of equity (ROE). I will save you the time and money to read that book. I read the entire book in an hour at Barnes and Noble's and it saved me some money / time, not to mention cutting down trees for that book. Basically it does not work today.

- DAL has an interesting Debt / Equity of over -1000% due to the negative equity. For a comparison, you may want to use Debt / ABS(Equity).

- Once in a while, I found the financial data was not consistent from different sources. Try to check out any discrepancy in the dates of the financial data of your sources. The financial statements from the company websites usually have the most updated data.

- Current Ratio = Current Asset / Current Liability. If it is below 1, then the company is having a tough time in meeting its current cash obligations.

- Dividend Yield is a valid metric for matured companies. I do not use it to evaluate growth companies or companies that need to plow back cash for research and development.

- If you use Finviz.com, you find three margins: profit, gross and operating. I prefer to use profit margin that is more useful for most companies. The other two may be relevant in some sectors.

  http://www.investopedia.com/terms/p/profitmargin.asp
  http://www.investopedia.com/terms/g/grossmargin.asp
  http://www.investopedia.com/terms/o/operatingmargin.asp

  Use Wikipedia for more description.

- Enron had millions in profits but negative cash flows. Earnings can be manipulated but not the cash flows.

  Insiders' selling usually does not cause any alarm unless excessively. Most insiders sell most of the stocks they have before these companies go bankrupt. Just common sense!

- Why fundamentals are important. (http://seekingalpha.com/article/1612442-its-shorting-season)

  On the same day when this article was published, RVLT was up 10% due to increasing sales in the earnings conference. However, the company is still not profitable. It shows how tough shorting is even with good arguments. That's why do not expect every purchase is profitable. However, with the educated guesses, you should beat the market in the long run.

- Due to my ignorance, limited time or my short period of holding stocks, I have not used intrinsic value that often.

  Book value is different from intrinsic value. Book value is calculated by summing up the values of all pieces of a company such as a building and all equipment.

  Intrinsic value is the real value of a company. When two companies have the same book value and market cap, the company that generates more profit than the other one usually has a higher intrinsic value. When the intrinsic value is higher than the stock price, it is underpriced in theory.

  The following link provides more info on intrinsic value.
  http://en.wikipedia.org/wiki/Intrinsic_value_%28finance%29

Testing key metrics

Here is a summary table on my findings in a recent test. It is based on a small amount data from 1-5-2007 to 1-7-2014 (about one market cycle). This is for illustrating how to test metrics and I am not responsible for any error in preparing the results.

Metric	P/E	PEG	P/S	P/FC	P/B
Criteria	<3	<1	<.06	<10	<2

I used P/E growth rate of P/E instead of PEG and it is 8%. My average P/S is about .07, substantially smaller than .8 from other tests.

If you have a historical database, you can test it out the above metrics and other metrics with the criteria described below.

Common testing criteria

The following are my basic criteria.

- Market Cap > 50 M.
- Price > 1 to reduce survivorship bias.
- Avg. Volume > 10,000.
- 3 Major Exchanges.
- EPS > 0. Only select stocks with positive earnings.

I started from 2007 and ended in 2013. I tested from the beginning of the year (actually with several days later due to no data on Jan. 1) to the end of the year. Repeat it for the next year and average the returns of all the 7 years. I call it 'window' testing to avoid the distorted value when you have a big win or loss in the early year.

To illustrate, I tested the above criteria with P/E and sort P/E in ascending order from 1/5/2007 to 1/4/2008. The top 10 stocks have an average of 44%. Repeated the test for the next 7 years.

Partial Result

Metric	P/E	PEG	P/S	SPY
Avg. Return	13%	8%	38%	6%
Beat SPY	124%	35%	538%	N/A

However, from my Market Timing book, I should be out of the stock market in second part of 2007 and the entire 2008. The next table is from 2009 to 2013 instead of from 2007 and resembles my actual trading better.

Metric	P/E	PEG	P/S	SPY
Avg. Return	35%	19%	125%	13%
Beat SPY	166%	45%	864%	N/A

The above metrics beat SPY by a larger percent in the 'good' years than the first table.

P/B and P/FC (Free Cash) are obtained info from other sources. I also had P/S Growth and it did not beat SPY. It is ignored. P/S turns out to be very important metric.

To illustrate such as the 3 in P/E, I selected the highest value of the P/E in the top 10 stocks for each year and averaged the values from 5 tests (from 2009).

Instead of holding the stocks for 1 year, I tried 2 years. The result is worse, so stick with holding the stocks for 1 year.

The next step is to find the best combination in more than one metric and their values, such as "P/S < .06" and "P/E < 3". If I do not find a lot of stocks, I would relax the criteria such as "P/S < .08 and "P/E < 4".

This is just a general guideline. Different sectors have different metrics. Super market has a very different P/S than high tech companies for example.

Technical indicators

Bring up finviz.com from your browser and enter the symbol of the stock.

Ensure the stock's SMA200 is above 0% as we do not want to buy stock in a downward trend. SMA200% is Single Moving Average for the last 200 trade sessions. The percent indicates how far the stock price from its SMA.

In addition, the RSI(14) should be less than 75, which would indicate the stock is overbought.

Summary table

Metric	Value	Indicates	Relaxed
Market: (use SPY)			
SMA350%	Above 0	Not plunging	Above 0
SMA350%	>9	Correction possible	>12
RSI(14)	>65	Correction possible	>70
Fundamentals:			
P/E	<4	Good	<8
PEG	<1	Good	<1.2
P/S	<.07	Good	<.8
Technical:			
SMA200%	>0	Up trend	>1
SMA200%	<10	Not peaking	<15
RSI(14)	<70	Not overbought	<75

#Filler: Why do poor countries remain poor?

One reason is suffering from repeated natural disasters such as earthquakes and hurricane.

Even the U.S. has been spending a lot of resources on Puerto Ricco, some politicians want to be kings and queens as they do not care about their citizens.

2   Finviz's parameters

Most metrics are described in Finviz (via Help), Investopedia and/or Wikipedia and my chapters on P/E and fundamental metrics if available. We use the metrics for screening stocks and then evaluating the screened stocks.

The following are my personal comments and why I feel some metrics are more important than the others. Personally I divide the metrics into fundamentals and technical, which are more important for long-term investors and short-term investors respectively.

Compare the ratios to the companies in the same sector (industry) and also its averages from the last few years (5 preferable) from many other websites such as Fidelity.

From your browser, enter Finviz.com. Enter a symbol (I used ABEO for discussion). A chart is displayed with the prices and volumes for the last eleven months. SMAs (Single Moving Average) are displayed sometimes with other technical indicators. Intraday, Daily and Weekly options are available for day traders, short-term traders and long-term traders respectively.

Besides the chart and the metrics described next, it describes what the company does, analysts' recommendations (I prefer Fidelity's Equity Summary), insiders' trading and articles that are good for intangible and qualitative analysis. Many free websites such as Yahoo!Finance may provide a list of articles about the company.

"Financial Highlights and Statements" are materials for more in-depth analysis and they were more important decades ago when most financial ratios had not been calculated for you. It is important for investors with good knowledge in financial accounting. The current version also includes basic financial statements and cash flow for the current (TTM) and the last two years.

A section on Insider Trading is also included. Do not be alarmed when insiders dump small quantities of the stocks. Buying large quantities (e.g. insider transaction more than 5%) at prices close to the market price could be favorable news.

The following metrics are roughly based on the flow of Finviz from top to bottom and left to right. I skip those metrics that I believe are not too important. You can also place your cursor on the metric to retrieve the description from Finviz. Some metrics are left blank to indicate they are not applicable (zero, negative or not available). For example, the Debt/Equity of YRCW in 1/2019 is blank (same as null) due to its negative Equity. From Yahoo!Finance at the time of writing, it has a total debt of 888M.

- **Index**. Most of us trade stocks in the three major exchanges in the USA. Stocks listed over-the-counter are too risky for most of us. Skip the stocks in local exchanges and foreign exchanges unless you are an expert on these stocks and/or have insightful (not insider) information. I screen the stocks and then ignore the stocks that are not in the Dow, NASDAQ and Amex. Other screeners may let you select a group of exchanges.

- **Market Cap** (MC). To me, stocks below 50M are risky even though they could be very profitable. Ensure the Avg. Volume is at least 10,000 shares and / or your order is less than 1% of the average volume. Some small stocks are controlled by the owners and have small volumes. In this case you cannot sell your stock easily.

  Float = Outstanding shares – Insider shares.

  Usually Float does not matter as they are typically the same. However, it does for small companies with large insider shares. Most of these owners do not want to sell their family businesses and hence they reduce the chance of being acquired entirely or partially for good prices. In this case, you may have to hold this stock for a long time or you sell it at a very unfavorable price.

- If **Forward P/E** (a.k.a. Expected P/E) is not provided, use the P/E which is based on the trailing last 12 months (TTM). Alternatively, calculate the E by using the E from P/E and multiplying it by its growth rate. It may not be seasonally adjusted. I prefer using Forward P/E as it provides a better predictability power to me.

  Finviz.com leaves the P/E blank (same as null) if the earnings are negative. In this case, I would check out Yahoo!Finance's EV /

EBITDA, which also considers taxes, cash and interests. The blank condition is similar to some metrics such as when the asset is negative (they seldom occur).

Earnings Yield is equal to E/P. I call it True Earnings Yield for EBITDA / EV. It is easier to understand. Compare Earnings Yield or True Yield to the annual dividend yield of a 10-year Treasury – with the low interest rate in 2021, skip the comparison.

E/P is easier in screening and sorting the screened stocks. If you use P/E instead of E/P, you need to screen or sort stocks with a clause "P/E > 0".

When the P/E is less than 5, be careful and there may be a reason why it is so low. Many bankrupting companies have low P/Es at one time.

Compare the P/E or Forward P/E with the average P/E for the sector and its average P/E for the last 5 years that are available from Fidelity.com. Some sectors have high P/Es. If the sector is cyclical, the earnings could be affected.

When the prospect of the company is good such as Tesla in 2020, ignore P/E.

- **Cash / share**. It is used to calculate Pow P/E and Pow EY when EV/EBITDA for the stock is not available. To illustrate, if the stock is $10 and it has $10 cash / share without debt (i.e. Debt/Equity = 0), most likely it is underpriced as you can get the whole company for nothing. You should find out why the price is so low. It could be the market ignoring the stock, or there is a serious event happening such as a major lawsuit.

- **Dividend %** is useful for income investors. The payout ratio should not be more than 30% except for matured companies. Most developing companies plough back the profits into research and development, and hence they do not pay dividends.

- **Recs**. Select stocks with 1 or 2. Do not base your stock selection on this recommendation alone. There have been many bad recommendations that could cost you a fortune in losses. Use Fidelity's Equity Summary Score instead.

- **PEG** is a measure of the growth of P/E and hence a growth metric. It is similar to P/E, but it takes the expected earnings growth rate into account. The lower value is better as long as earnings are positive. If earnings are negative, then the reverse is true. It is a defect in using P/E and PEG and that's why I recommend EY (Earnings Yield) and EYG, earnings yield growth.

  If there are two companies with the same P/E, the one with a better PEG ratio is better. If two companies have the same E/P, the company with higher Earnings Growth (EPS Q/Q) would be better for similar logic.

- **P/B**. Book value (= Total Assets – Total Liabilities) may not include intangible assets such as patents. Do not trust it 100%, so is ROE which is based on the book value. Negative equity is possible when Total Liabilities is more than Total Assets. This popular metric is outdated for most matured companies as it is now made up of more intangible assets including patents, management, the quality of their employees, brand names, market share, partners, free cash flow and customer base.

- **P/S**. If two companies are unprofitable, this ratio can be used. A retail company such as Walmart is very different from a research company. This metric is only meaningful for stocks within the same sector or specific sectors.

- **P/FCF**. I prefer it to be greater than 0 and less than 50 for value investors. Most metrics can be manipulated easily, but not this one.

- **Sales Q/Q** reduces the seasonal deviation. To illustrate, retail sales for the Christmas season should be compared to the same season in the prior year.

- **EPS Q/Q**. Same as above. I prefer the growth of EPS over Sales. Both of these Q/Q ratios are growth metrics. When a company terminates its unprofitable product(s), its Sales Q/Q could be down but its EPS Q/Q could be up. In 2000, many internet companies had great Sales Q/Qs but negative EPS Q/Qs.

Q/Q comparison (quarter to quarter) takes out the seasonal variations as Sales Q/Q. I prefer both Sales Q/Q and EPS Q/Q increase. When EPS Q/Q increases far higher than Sales Q/Q, it could mean the EPS Q/Q could be temporary such as the oil company when the oil price rockets.

When the company buys its own shares, EPS could be misleading as E is fixed and the number of shares is reduced. In most cases, the fundamentals of the company have not changed.

- Positive **Insider** Transactions are favorable. Sometimes, they are misleading. Need to scroll to the end of the screen and check out more info there. If the transactions are outdated such as 3 months or so ago, and or they are purchases in a similar amount than the sales a while ago, they are not important. Insiders know the company better than us. So is Institutional Transactions as institutional investors move the market.

- Insider Own, Shares Outstanding and Shares **Float** determine the number of shares that are available for trading. A small Float with a high Insider Own limits trading and the stock should be avoided in most cases. Compare your trade position for the stock to the Avg. Volume.

- **Profit Margin**. I prefer it over Gross Margin and Oper. Margin which does not include interest expenses and taxes. When you sell software, the Gross Margin is high as it does not include development, support and marketing, etc. A retail store has low Gross Margin. It all depends on the industry, and hence it is better to compare companies in the same industry.

- **Short Float**. I prefer it to be less than 10%. If it is greater than 10%, the shorters could find something wrong with the company. If it is over 25% (indicating a possible short squeeze), I would check the fundamentals. If they are good, I would buy expecting a short squeeze potential. It is risky but it has been proven to be profitable for me.

- Technical metrics: SMA-20, SMA-50 and SMA-200. Finviz expresses them in convenient percentages. If they are all positive, it means the trend is up. SMA-20 and SMA-50 are a short-term trend and SMA-200 is a long-term trend. If you are a short-term swing investor, stick with the short-term trend and vice versa. The first two are also used as momentum grades. Many long-term investors do not buy stocks when the SMA-200% is negative.

- **RSI(14)**. If it is greater than 65%, it is overbought. If it is under 30%, it is under-bought for me. Some use 5% up or down than mine. Use it as a reference. Most stocks making new heights are always overbought, and many of these stocks keep on rising. I recommend using trailing stops to protect your profit.

- **Beta**. A volatile stock fluctuates a lot. It is good for short-term traders. A beta of 1 means the stock would fluctuate with the market, and be volatile if it is higher than 1. For volatile stocks (higher than 1), the stops should be higher. For example, if your stops are normally 15%, you may want to use 20% or even higher.
- Management performance is measured by ROE. It is also judged by **Analysts' Rec.** and Institutional Ownership (except for small companies). The confidence of their own ability, the company and its sector is measured by Insider Ownership and Insider Purchases.

  ROE = Net Income / Average Shareholder's Equity
  According to Investopedia, a normal ROE for utilities should be 10% while high tech companies should be 15%. Compare this ratio and many other ratios with its peers that are available from Fidelity.
- Avoid all companies that are going to bankrupt at all costs. Debt/Equity, P/FCF, Cash/Sh., P/B, Profit Margin, Forward P/E, Short Float, RSI(14), SMA20% and SMA50 would give us hints. Need to summarize all the info and study many other factors such as obsoleting products (including drugs).
- Unless you have concrete information, do not buy stocks a week or so before the Earnings Date. It is seldom to make great profits when the announcement is better than the expected.

More useful information:
- The price chart. It has a lot of features such as the resistance line. Some charts include technical indicators such as double top (a bearish warning) and double bottom (a bullish sign).

- Description under the symbol. It briefly describes what the company (sector and industry) does and its country of registration. You want to buy a stock within a sector that is trending up. For example, according to Finviz Apple is in the Consumer Goods sector and the Electronic Equipment industry.

  If you do not want to buy foreign stocks, skip it if it is not listed in the US exchange.
- Articles on the company for qualitative analysis.
- Insider trading. Pay more attention to the insider purchases at market prices. Use common sense.
- The last line lets you open Yahoo!Finance and other sites.

Other important sites

Yahoo!Finance.

From Statistics, you can find Enterprise Value / EBITDA. I call it True Yield when I flip them to EBITDA / Enterprise Value.

In case it is not available, I use Earnings Yield. In my spreadsheet without considering the cell designations,

=IF (Earnings Yield = "", True Yield, Earnings Yield)

Fidelity
Compare the P/E of the average PE of the last 5 years. In my spreadsheet for demonstration,

Cheaper By Historically =IF(PE="","",(Avg. of 5-year PE -PE)/Avg. of 5-year PE)

Compare the P/E of companies in the same sector. In my spreadsheet for demonstration,

Cheaper By To the peers =IF(PE="","",(Industry PE - PE)/Industry PE)

Your broker's website

Your broker website should have plenty of tools to analyze stocks. As of Dec., 2018, Fidelity lets you use their extensive research free by opening an account with no position restriction. I describe some of their metrics that should be beneficial to your research.

- Equity Summary Score. Potentially good buy when it is 7 (8 for conservative investors) or higher. With some exceptions, you should avoid or short stocks if the score is 3 or below. The stocks ranking from 4 to 6 could be turnaround candidates if they are supported by good Q/Q Earnings and/or good news.

- The 5-year averages are good yardsticks. For example, in Dec., 2018, C's P/E is about 9 and the average is 14. Hence it is a value buy.

Other sources

If you have other sources (most require a subscription or being a customer), skip the stocks that have one of the failing grades. The exceptions are a new positive development and increased insider purchases.

Vendor	Grade	Fail
Fidelity	Equity Summary Score	< 7
IBD	Composite grade	< 50
Value Line	Proj. 3-5 yr. return. Also its composite rating	< 3%
Zacks	Rank	5
VectorVest	VST	< 0.7

You may be able to find Value Line and IBD in your library. Try out the free stock reports from your broker first. Finviz and Seeking Alpha should have articles (now fewer free articles from Seeking Alpha) on stocks and earnings conferences, which could have important information after separating from the "welcome" and garbage talks.

Yahoo!Finance has good info. "EV/EBITDA" is better than "P/E" as it considers debts and cash. Most use Earnings from last 12 months, which has poorer predictability than Forward Earnings to me.

When negative values such as Equity in Finviz.com, we need to adjust many related metrics or do not use them at all.

MarketWatch.com has many articles on the market in general and personal investing.

If the stock is close to the Earnings Date (found in Finviz.com), you should avoid trading the stock; as earnings could have a big swing for the stock price. Consult Zacks' ranking which is currently free for individual stocks.

Gurus

It is nice to know how gurus would rate the interested stocks. GuruFocus is a good source. NASDAQ is a simplified version, but it is currently free. Bring up Nasdaq.com from your browser. Select "Investing" and then "Guru Screeners". On the third selection, enter the stock symbol such as THO. Click "Go". You will find how 10 or so gurus would evaluate this stock in theory. Click "Detailed Analysis" for each guru.

Quick and dirty

Many times we need to evaluate a stock fast such as taking action due to some development. Refer to my other article "Simplest way to evaluate stocks". The following should take a few minutes. Bring up Finviz.com and enter the stock symbol.

Using SWKS on 6/10/16 to illustrate, Forward P/E is about 11 (fine between 3 and 25), Debt/Eq. is 0 (fine less than .5), ROE is 30% (fine greater than 5%) and P/PCF is 31 (fine if not negative).

Also, check out Market Cap, Avg. Volume, Dividend, Short Float (fine between 0% and 10%), Country and Industry. Judging from the above, it is a buy.

If you have more time, check out the following: Recom. (Ok if less than 2.5), P/B (fine between .5 and 4), Sales Q/Q (fine if not negative), EPS Q/Q (fine if not negative), Cash/Sh (compare it to Debt/Sh) and Profit Margin (fine >5%). Check some articles described for this stock.

5-minute stock evaluation

It takes even less time than the above "Quick and Dirty". However, I recommend you should spend more time researching stocks.

- From Finviz.com, enter the stock or ETF symbol. Look at the number of reds in metrics. If there are more than greens, most likely it is not a good stock.

- It should be fine if Fidelity's Equity Summary Score is greater than 8.

If you have more time, I recommend you to check the following:

- Check out Forward P/E (E>0 and P/E < 20), Debut / Equity (< 50%) and P/FCF (not in red color).

  If time is allowed, replace Forward P/E with True P/E (same as "EV/EBITDA"), which is available from Yahoo!Finance and other sources.

- SMA20 (or SMA50 for longer holding period). If SMA20 is > 10%, it is trending up.

- It is fine if the Insider Transaction is positive.

- Be cautious on foreign stocks and low-volume stocks.
- If most of the above are positive, it is likely a buy. As in life, nothing is 100% certain.

Links
PEG: http://en.wikipedia.org/wiki/PEG_ratio
Short %:
http://www.investopedia.com/university/shortselling/shortselling1.asp#a
xzz2LNDvpemo
Openinsider: http://www.openinsider.com/
Finviz: http://Finviz.com/
terms: http://www.Finviz.com/help/screener.ashx
Insider Cow: http://www.insidercow.com/
Current Ratio: http://en.wikipedia.org/wiki/Current_ratio
How to find quality stocks.
http://seekingalpha.com/article/2381395-how-to-identify-quality-stocks-
and-is-there-really-alpha-to-be-had

3 Mysteries of P/E

If you believe you can make good money by selecting stocks with low P/Es solely, dream on. If it were that easy, there would be no poor folks. However, buying fundamentally sound companies would reduce the risk and improve the chance of its appreciation.

P/E is the most misunderstood indicator. To me, it is the most useful one among all metrics if it is properly used. Earnings are the key to stock appreciation and P/E measures its value. To illustrate on P/E, you pay a million for a hot-dog cart in NYC. Even if its earnings increase year after year, you will never recoup your investment as you have paid too much even for a good business.

"Buy stocks with P/E below 15 and earnings positive" is not true in many cases. P/E growth (PEG) should be considered at least as a prospect of the company. Many retailers were destroyed by Amazon and many newspapers were destroyed by Facebook and Google. Which sector do you want to buy: the sector in up trending or the dying sector even with a better P/E?

Most old books on value are based on old industries that are no longer applicable in today's market. Read these books but ask the above question.

Better definition
P/E should be inverted as E/P, which is termed as Earnings Yield. Earnings Yield is easy to be compared and understood. It takes care of negative earnings for screening stocks and ranking (comparing stocks with the better P/E first). If you sort P/E in ascending order, your order will be wrong with the negative earnings but right with E/P.

It is usually compared to a 10-year Treasury bill yield (or 30 years) or a CD rate. If the stock has 5% earnings yield and your one-year CD is 1%, then it beats the CD by 4% in absolute numbers and four times better. However, the CD is virtually risk free (with deposit amount limits in most banks). Earning yield is an estimated guess and it may not materialize.

Many ways to predict E/P
- Based on the last 12 months. Project it to the Forward E/P. It is also called the last twelve month E/P.

- Based on analysts' educated guesses. Guesses may not materialize. Based on my experience, the expected usually predicts better than the one based on the last 12 months. This is the one I use most and many investing subscriptions provide this Forward P/E (same as the Expected P/E) or expected E/P.

Usually I do not trust the analyst's opinions due to their conflict of interest. However, the earnings estimate is my exception.

- Based on the last month or the last quarter. Latest information could be better for predictions. However, they are not good for seasonal businesses such as the retail where most sales are done during the Christmas season.
- Besides the Pow PE described later, I take the average of the earnings yield EY as:

The Avg. EY = (EY from the last twelve month + Expected EY + EY from the current month of prior year) / 3

It averages out using figures from the past, the present and the future. If no one has used it, I claim shamelessly it is my original idea.

Best E/P could not be the best
Very high E/P could be signs of troubles ahead such as a lawsuit pending, fraud, etc. If you find companies E/P over 50%, it means two years' profits could be equal to the entire cost of the company! I can tell you right away that they probably smell fishy unless you believe that there is a free lunch in life.

However, from time to time, some bargains do exist due to certain conditions, or the Wall Street is just wrong about the company. I found one in my year-end screen and that gave me huge return. You need to find out whether they are bargains or traps. When the E/P is low (sometimes even negative) but is improving fast, it could mean big profits for you. Fundamentalists may miss this opportunity in the early stages due to the unfavorable E/P, but it could be the most profitable time to buy. Sometimes, it could be a turnaround.

During a recession, most good companies have a hard time in promoting new products as the consumers are thrifty. At the same time, it usually is the best time to develop products if they have enough cash to finance them. In this case, there will be no alarm even with negative earnings. The only alarm is when a company cannot meet the debt obligations.

Some companies can manipulate earnings via dirty tricks in accounting. It could make this year look really good, but it is harder or even impossible to continue the same trick for many years. Check out the footnotes in the financial statement.

E/P and PEG

For value investing, E/P is usually used and the higher the better. Watch out when it is extraordinarily high.

PEG (P/E growth) measures the rate of improving P/E. '1' is supposed to be neutral to most investors. When it is below 1, it is undervalued, and vice versa.

PEG = (P/E) / Earnings Growth Rate

They have a similar problem with P/E with negative earnings.

Which of the following two stocks do you want to buy based on their historical earning yields and earnings growth?

1. A stock that has a 10% earnings yield with no earnings growth.
2. A stock that has an 8% earnings yield with 50% earnings growth.

If the earnings growth continues, in next year the second stock should pay 12%, substantially better than the first stock. This is another reason we should use forward earnings rather than historical earnings.

PEG may give a low value for companies that pay high dividends. To correct it,

PEG = (P/E)/ (Earning Growth Rate + Dividend Yield)

When the general market favors growth stocks, weigh more on growth metrics including PEG. I claim no credit on the adjusted PEG.

Fundamental metrics

E/P is one of the metrics you should use but not exclusively. If the earning yield is high but the % of debt is high too, then a good bargain may not be as good as it appears to be.

Some other metrics may not be easily found in the financial statements such as the intangibles, insider buying, pension obligations, trade secrets, losing market share, brand name, customers' loyalty, etc. It is interesting that most metrics change its ability to predict from time to time.

P/E variations

There are other P/E variations like Shiller P/E (same as CAPE and PE10). Shiller P/E can also be used to track the current market valuation. It is controversial and its value is easily misinterpreted. Hence, use it as a reference only unless you understand all its issues. I prefer to use two year average of the P/E instead of 10 as I believe the market changes too much over a ten year span. Currently Shill P/E does not work that well as before. It is due to the excessive printing of money.

Compare a company's current P/E to its average P/E in the last 5 years. Also compare it to the average value of the companies in the same industry. The average P/E for high-tech companies is different from supermarkets for example. They are available from Fidelity.

P/E is more reliable for a group of stocks (SPY for example) instead of individual stocks which have too many other metrics and intangibles to deal with. When you compare the total return of an ETF to a corresponding index, you need to add the respective dividends to the index to ensure a fair comparison of total returns. As of this writing, the S&P 500 is paying about a 2% dividend.

EV/EBITDA is another way to measure the value of a company. This metric has its advantages and disadvantages over P/E. It includes other important data such as cash and debt. EBITDA/EV is equivalent to E/P including other mentioned metrics. I prefer to use it over E/P. Some sites do not provide it if the earnings is negative. The disadvantage to me is it does not use expected earnings. This ratio can be found under Yahoo!Finance.

Garbage in, garbage out
I do not trust most financial statements from emerging countries, especially the smaller companies. Watch out for fraudulent data.

Most metrics can be manipulated. Recently I have a US stock that lost 18% in one day due to the SEC's investigation of its financial data.

The announced earnings may not be reflected in the financial statements that you use from the web. Ensure your data is up-to-date by checking the date of the financial statements. Seeking Alpha has transcripts for the earnings announcements that would save you a trip to attend the companies' quarterly meetings.

Sector and entire market

You can find the value of a sector using the P/E of an ETF for that sector. It is similar for the market. For example, use SPY (an ETF simulating the S&P 500 index). If it is lower than the average (15 to me), then most likely the market is good value and a buy signal. It is one of the many hints for market timing.

Where to use P/E

Each highlight of the following corresponds to one of my books. Click it for the description of the strategy.

My book on top-down approach starts with a safe market, then sector analysis, fundamental analysis, intangible analysis and optionally technical analysis. P/E is one of the many metrics in fundamental analysis.

There are many styles of investing. In general, fundamental analysis is important when you hold the stock longer.

- P/E is important in Long-Term Swing, Dividend Investing, Retirees and Conservative Strategies.
- My max value is 20 and 25 for tech companies. I ignore it if they have high potential for appreciation that could be indicated by insider purchases. However, many unknown companies then had a P/E over 50. Tesla had a P/E over 1,000 at one time.
- P/E is moderately important in Short-Term Swing and Sector Rotation.
- P/E is the least important in Momentum Strategy and Day Trading.

Summary

Again, one metric should not dictate the reason to trade a stock. Compare the company P/E to its industry average and its own five-year average. In addition, many industries have cycles. If you buy it at the peak of the industry, the P/E may mislead you. Besides fundamental analysis, you need to consider intangible analysis and time the entry / exit point by using technical analysis. Intangible analysis evaluates information that cannot be summarized into numeric metrics such as a lawsuit pending.

True P/E

"EV/EBITDA" is available from Yahoo!Finance and other sources. The true EY is "1/Ture PE". I call it "True" for the lack of a better term as it represents the financial situation of the company better. This could be the most important metric for many.

Earnings can be manipulated. For example, the company management can lower the P/E ratio by buying back its stocks. In this case the earnings per share is boosted but in reality there is no change in the company's financial fundamentals. The true P/E takes into consideration the reduced cash. EBITBA stands for "Earnings Before Interest, Taxes, Depreciation, and Amortization".

Be careful when EV or "EBITDA" is negative. Most likely you should avoid the stocks with a negative EV.

Yahoo!Finance usually leaves EV/EVITDA blank for financial institutions such banks, loan companies and REITS. In this case, use forward earnings yield (= 1 / Forward P/E or Pow Earnings Yield described next.

Pow P/E

You should use the described "EV/EBITDA" and hence "Pow P/E" can be ignored. There are some cases that Pow P/E is better: 1. "EV/EBITDA" may not be available for reasons such as negative asset and 2. Use of Forward Earnings instead of Earnings based on the last twelve months. The following is an exercise on how I simulate it from Finviz.com with metrics that are readily available.

I modified P/E to take care of cash and debts. I use my last name due to being easier to distinguish from P/E and it has nothing to do with my ego.

Pow P/E = (P - Cash per Share + Debt per Share) / (Earning - Interest gained per share - Interest paid per share)

Pow Earnings Yield = 1 / Pow P/E

Here is a comparison of E/P (Earnings Yield), Expected Earnings Yield (Forward E /P), True Yield (EBITD/EV) and Pow Earning Yields, which is based one Forward (Expected) Earnings as of 10/14/2021.

	CARS	MPAA
Earnings Yield	1%	7%
Expected Earnings Yield	12%	12%
True Yield	13%	11%
Pow Earnings Yield	5%	9%

P/E is not always important

The following is my test from 1/2/2020 to 10/14/2020. RSP is similar to SPY except that the stocks in the S&P 500 index are equally weighed. EY (= E/P) is Expected Earnings Yield and there is no stocks with EY less than 0. DY is Dividend Yield. GPE is the growth of P/E. As in my book, I use annualized returns and dividends are not included. This test does not mean a lot, but it tells us what these metrics behave during this period, or it indicates **Value is not a good metric in this period**, and it may indicate momentum is better in this period. Most big winners start as small companies with **high P/E** (from 30 to 100). Many of them have important technologies or special systems that would change the world such as Microsoft, Facebook, Amazon and Walmart to name a few. Their sales have increased substantially year after year.

Examples of not depending on low P/Es. Before the financial crisis in 2008, P/Es of most bank stocks had 10-year low. After they announced the earnings, P/Es of many of them surged to over 100 and the stock prices suffered losses of more than 80% within 12 months. The stock price of Bethlehem Steel with P/E of 2 at one time went to zero. Need to find out why the stock is so cheap via intangible analysis and qualitative analysis.

The following is very rough testing and there are many limitations in the database. However, the conclusion is quite convincing to me and some are opposite to the contrary beliefs. For example, I expected the higher EY the better, but not in this test.

	Ann. Return	Indicator	Comment
RSP 500 All	-2%		
EY (top 10)	-54%	Bad	Contrary
GPE (top 10)	-20%	Bad	Contrary
Select All or top 100.			
DY = 0	16%	Good	
DY (top 100)	-19%	Bad	
DY / 1 and 2	2%		
EY 3 to 4	15%	Good	Second best
EY 2 to 3	6%	Good	Third best
EY 1 to 2	31%	Good	Best
EY 0 to 1	-39%	Bad`	

I use some metrics from a service I subscribe to that are not included here. Two major metrics of this subscription have a return of around 20%. Most subscriptions including the free Fidelity (to some extent) give you three composite scores: Total, Fundamental and Timing. I wish to check out the recent predictability of Fidelity's Equity Summary Score if they have a historical database. Most of them take out the delisted and /or bankrupt companies in their databases. Link: P/E: https://www.youtube.com/watch?v=4KkTGx2bK_4

4   Intangibles

I give a score for each stock I evaluate. Occasionally some stocks with poor scores have great returns and vice versa. In general, the scoring system works. It has been proven statistically and repeatedly from my limited data. I stick with high-score stocks with some exceptions.

Once in a while I change my scoring system to adept to the current market conditions. To illustrate, the market bottom phase and early recovery phase of the market cycle favor value more than momentum/growth. Here are some of my recent experiences and strategies:

- I double or even triple my stake on stocks with high scores. In the longer term, they are consistently better winners than the average with some minor exceptions. Besides the score, look at the intangibles described in this article.

- Watch out for the stocks with outrageous metrics such as P/E of 4 or less. It could be a big lawsuit pending, an expiration of some important drugs, etc. Also, be careful with scores in the top 5%. From my statistics they do worse than the average. Their problems may not show up in the current financial statements.

- The technology of a tech company cannot be ignored even though the company's P/E is high, that I set a limit of 25 instead of 20 for other stocks. The value of the company's technology and patents will not be shown in the fundamental metrics except from the insiders' purchases at market prices.

  For example, IDCC rose about 40% in 2 days. There was a rumor that Google was buying the company and/or Apple was bidding on it too for its mobile technology. Charts usually would flag this kind of event. For non-charters, use the SMA-20% from Finviz.com. They could be a little late as the charts depend on rising prices.

- There are more acquisitions during a market bottom (same as early recovery). The companies with good technologies are bargains and the larger companies especially those in the same sector understand their values better than most of us. These potentially profitable companies will not be shown by their scores explicitly. When corporations have a lot of cash or the credit is cheap, they are looking for smaller companies to acquire or invest in. The candidates are usually small, beaten up, low-priced and having valuable intangible assets such as technologies, customer base and/or market share of the industry segment. 2009-2012 was just the perfect environment and the before that was 2003. I had at least one stock in each of these periods and they appreciated a lot.

- The opposite is Netflix, Chipotle in 1/2012 and Amazon in 1/2013. They are over-priced by any measure. However, the mentioned companies are investing in the future. The shorters (not for beginners) are having a tough time in making money on them. When their P/Es are higher than 40, watch out. Some could be OK in the mentioned companies, but usually they are not. Do not follow the herd and your due diligence will verify whether they will still go up.

Use reward/risk ratio. It is based on experiences. To illustrate, if the company has the equal chance to go up 50% and go down 25%, then it is a buy and the reverse is a sell.

- The retail investor just cannot possibly know about some events until they actually happen. For example, ATSC dropped 15% due to losing its second primary customer. Fundamentals cannot predict this kind of events. Charts can signal this event, but usually they are too late unless you watch the chart all day long.

- After a quick run up, TZOO plunged due to missing some negligible earning expectations. It seems the original climbing prices already had the perfect earnings growth built-in.

  I do not understand why a company loses 10% of its market cap when it missed by 1% of the expected earnings. It could be driven up and down by the institutional investors. Evaluate the stock before you act. Acting opposite to the institutional investors could be very profitable for the right stocks. Avoid trading before the earnings announcement dates (about 4 times a year for most stocks).

- The following are not easily found in financial statements: industry outlook, patents, good will, market share, competition, product margins, management quality, lawsuits pending, potential acquisition, pension obligations, advertising icons, etc. That is why we need to read articles on the stocks in our buy list or our purchased stocks.

- The financial data could be fraudulent or manipulated. I do not trust small companies in emerging markets. I have been burned too many times. Check the company names such as foreign names, ADR and their headquarter addresses (from the company profile in most investing sites).

  Earnings can be manipulated with many accounting tricks. A jump in earnings from last year may not be as rosy as it looks.

Check the footnotes in the accounting statements. I usually skip financial statements unless I have big purchases in mind as my time in investing is limited.

- Cash flow cannot be easily manipulated. It is good information whether the company will survive or not, but to me it does not prove to be a consistent predictor in my tests, but an important red flag for companies on their way to bankruptcy. Examples abound.

- Repeated one-time, non-recurring and extraordinary charges are red flags.

- Stay away from the companies where the CEOs are over-compensated. As of 7- 2013, Activision's CEO raised his salary by more than 600%, while the stock lost its value in double digits.

- Value stocks. Need to know why they become value stocks (i.e. fewer investors want to own) even they are financially sound. For example, there are two primary reasons for the downfall of a supplier to Apple: 1. Apple is declining in sales and 2. Apple is switching suppliers to replace their product. Technology companies are continually building better mouse traps. They could turn around in a year or so with better products.

Conclusion

Buying a stock is an educated guess that its stock price will rise. Fundamentals do not always work, but they work most of the time:

1. When we buy a value stock, we're swimming against the tide. Hence, we need to wait longer (usually more than 6 months) for the market to realize its value. The exception is the Early Recovery phase (see the Market Cycle chapter) and it has faster and larger returns than most other stocks from most other stages of the market cycle.

2. Some metrics are misleading. Book value could be misleading for an established company such as IBM. The image of the cowboy in a tobacco company could be a very important asset that is not included in its financial statement.

3. The market is not always rational.

Afterthoughts

- Brand names of big companies are one of the most important intangibles. Here is a strategy to buy big companies in a down market. It has been proven that it works. However, do not just buy these companies without analysis.
  http://seekingalpha.com/article/1324041-buying-brand-names-in-a-bear-market-can-make-you-rich

- The reputation of a company takes a long time to build but a bad incidence to destroy in the case of GM such as the delay in recalling the killer switches.

#Filler: Carrie Fisher, another sad American story

Unless drug addiction is part of the culture now as evidenced from the legalization of certain drugs, we're in a permissive society! Brits pushed opium as a nation when they had nothing better to trade. Opium killed millions of Chinese and bankrupted China. When we do not learn from history, we will repeat history. It is another sad story of fame and money and then losing it all. I bet she would be happier in a normal life instead of being born in a privileged class. Same can be said for many celebrities such as Presley, Houston and her daughter. RIP.

5   Qualitative analysis

This is the last analysis to evaluate a stock fundamentally. Then the next is technical analysis which is used to find an entry point (also the exit point) for the stock.

Where quantitative analysis fails and why

I find that some stocks with high scores fail and some stocks with low scores succeed as indicated by my performance monitor. The scoring system still works statistically for the majority of my stocks.

- Reasons why stocks with low scores perform in addition to the described in the last discussion:

    - Over-sold. The institutional investors (fund managers and pension managers) dump them first, and then followed by the retail investors. These big boys will buy these stocks back when they reach a certain price range. RSI(14), a technical indicator described in the Technical Analysis article, is useful to detect these over-sold stocks. This metric is readily available from many sites including Finviz.

    - The falling price (P) improves all fundamental metrics that have the stock price such as P/E and P/Sales. However, the trend of the price is down.

    - The company has turned around after fixing its problems and/or the market has changed for the better.

    - The current problems have been resolved but not known to the public. It includes resolving a lawsuit, a new product, a new drug, or a new big order, etc.

    - Heavy purchases by insiders. The company's outlook is not shown in its financial statements. Sometimes the insiders hide them so they can buy more of their companies' stocks for themselves.

- Reasons why stocks with high scores plunge in addition to the described in the previous discussion:

- The company's fundamentals and its prices have reached or closed to the maximum heights. They have no way to go but down. It is particularly true when the stock's timing rating is at or close to the highest point. TTWO that I gifted to my grandchildren had been 5-baggers in the last few years before it plunged in 2018.

- It has reached its potential value (or a target price) and it is time for many investors to take profits.

- Sector (or stock) rotation, particularly by institutional investors who drive the market.

- The outlook of the company, its sector and/or the market is deteriorating.

- The stock price may be manipulated. There are many reasons to pump and dump the stock. Shorting is not recommended for most investors. However, some experienced shorters make money consistently when they find valid reasons to short stocks.

- It could be due to a new serious lawsuit, a new competing product or drug, canceling a major order, etc.

- Downgrade by analysts. They could spot some bad events such as product defects, violations of regulations or accounting errors / frauds. The downgrades are more important than the upgrades that could have conflict of interest.

- The financial statement had been manipulated. The SEC may ask for an investigation.

- Does not meet the consensus in earnings announcements, which have been over-acted by many investors.

Qualitative Analysis

We need to do further analysis after the quantitative analysis and the intangible analysis. Check out the company's prospects. Check out the date of the article and any potential hidden agenda items from the author. Older articles may not have much value.

Be careful on 'pump-and-dump' manipulation written by authors with a hidden agenda. It has happened especially on small companies before even SeekingAlpha.com has its share. Here was an article that tells you to sell NHTC. There was another article to tell you to buy ARTX. They fit into this category.

The sources are:

1. Seeking Alpha.
    Type the symbol of the company to read as many articles on the company as you have time for. Today this site and many other similar sites require you to be a paid member. If you cannot find too many good articles, check out the articles from Finviz.com.

    Recently, I read an article on AMD and it said it may have good profits in the next two years with the game consoles. The outlook of a company is not shown by any fundamental metric which are far from favorable.

    Following a well-known writer, I bought IBM without doing my due diligence (my fault). It went down more than 15% quickly. You can learn from my mistakes.

2. Research reports from your broker. If you do not find many, open an account with one that provides such reports. Some subscription services such as Value Line provide such reports.

3. Yahoo!Finance board. Most comments are garbage. However, once in a while you find some great insights. Usually you cannot find any info from other sources on tiny companies.

4. The most recent company's financial statements. They are usually available in the company's web site.

5. 10-Ks from Edgar database (www.sec.gov/edgar). Check out new products and its potential competition, key customers, order backlog, research and development and pending lawsuits.
6. Check out the outlook of the sector the company is in and the company itself.

7. Check out its competitors.
8. Some companies are run by stupid people. I received information via my email saying that my mutual fund account could be treated as an abandoned property. I have been cashing dividend checks every year and why it would be considered as an abandoned property. I called them right away to close my account.

   The tall and handsome guy presented articulately how he would turn around JC Penny on TV. I could tell you right away that all his tricks had been tried by other companies such as Sears, and most did not work. The intelligent investor does not care about how handsome, how articulated, how rich his family is and how many advanced degrees from prestigious colleges he possesses. If he does not make sense, do not buy his preaching and his company's stock. [Update. As of 5/2020, J.C. Penny filed for bankruptcy protection. If you had this stock and my book, you would have saved a lot of money minus $10 for my book!]

9. Check out its business model. Some business models do not make business sense and some do. Here are some samples.
- Giving razors makes sense, as the customers have to buy the blades eventually and keep on buying blades for life.
- Supermarket M lowers prices on common merchandises such as Coke and it works. They make money by providing inferior (but profitable to them) products that you cannot compare prices easily such as meat and seafood.

  Eventually there will be a supermarket in my area to satisfy me both in price and quality or at least make a good tradeoff.

- Last week it had been brutally hot. I went to a Barns & Noble's bookstore to enjoy reading the updated books and enjoyed the air conditioning. When there are more free loaders like me than customers, this business model does not work.
- Market dumping works to capture the market. Microsoft used to do it with their new Office and Mail products that could not compete with the established products at the time. Google is following the same model to dump its equivalent products to compete with Office. Now, Microsoft is taking a dose of the same medicine.

6   Manipulators and bankruptcy

If we can avoid bankrupting companies and/or companies losing most of their stock values, our portfolio would be improved substantially. Some companies make bad bets and lose, such as Enron betting on energy futures. Here are some signs of bad situations.

- Foreign companies. I do not have too much luck in developing countries especially their stocks of small companies. They include China, Ireland and Israel to name a few. However, as of 2019, many large Chinese companies are doing very well.
- When the P/E is too good, find out why. If the P/E is too bad, stay away.
- P/PFC should be greater than 0 and less than 50. Even a healthy cash flow may not be able to service the debt if it is huge. Hence, compare the cash flow to Debt/Equity.
- Altman Z-Score. I prefer a score above 3, a sign not to be bankrupted. However, Z-Score is not designed for financial sectors.
- Beneish M-Score. I prefer a score less than -2.22, a sign that the earnings are not manipulated. Both Z-Score and M-Score are available from GuruFocus.com for a fee.
- Z-Score metrics are: "Working Capital / Total Assets" (A), "Retained Earnings / Total Assets" (B), "Earnings Before Interest & Taxes / Total Assets" (C), "Market Cap / Total Liabilities" (D) and "Sales / Total Assets" (E).
  Z-Score = 1.2 A + 1.4 B + 3.3 C +.6 D + E
- Skip companies with bond ratings less than B.
- New government regulations such as taking out the credit for solar panels.
- Extraordinary profits such as Timber Liquidator and many banks in 2007-2008.
- Accounting manipulation: Excessive buying of stocks to boost Earnings per Share, excessive loans to officers, companies betting on futures such as Enron, too many one-time charges and reinstating the previous earnings.
- Skip thinly-traded stocks especially those stocks with the majority owned by a few owners.

The current financial statements could be the best source to look for them. If you read something you do not understand, be cautious.

We need to consistently monitor our stock holdings and sell them before they lose most of their value. I Recommend use stops.

This is why we need to have a focused investment portfolio of about 10 stocks; the number depends on your time available for investing. To illustrate, I have about 10 stocks with larger investments and about 100 stocks in smaller purchases. I would likely spend more time in monitoring the 10 stocks than the rest.

Mergers

Mergers are usually good for the merging companies to eliminate duplicate corporate functions such as payroll administration and researching on similar subjects.

The company being acquired usually has a high appreciation. I have a screen to search for the potential candidates. The Early Recovery (a phase of the market cycle defined by me) has more of these candidates. Big companies know their values and see good values when these stocks have been beaten in the market.

Then I do an intangible analysis on items that are not available from the financial statements and/or cannot be quantified. They are patents, technologies, researches, customer base, brand name, barriers to entry, distribution channels, competition, product cycle, management and pension obligations.

In 2003 I bought stock in a software company that was acquired by IBM profiting more than double. In the 2008 cycle, I bought ALU at $1 and sold it shortly at 40% profit. I expected Cisco would acquire it as Cisco did not build network. Cisco and actually U.S. did not acquire this valuable technology. In two years it was acquired by another competitor for more than $3. I need patience.

The company going to be acquired tries to make the financial statements look very rosy. A Chinese company tricked Caterpillar in acquiring it and Caterpillar lost huge in this deal. Even big company can be fooled. The record mergers in 2015 may not be good for the companies involved judging from the past history. When two losing companies merge, there will be one big loser.

7   Avoid bankrupting companies

Avoid the bankrupting companies at all costs. Here are some hints that a company is going bankrupt:

- I had several companies that had lost most of their stock values. It turns out that most were Chinese companies. I did have some losers from Mexico, Israel and Ireland. I believe most were set up to cheat investors. Most if not all had 'rosy' financial statements. Avoid them, especially small companies in emerging countries.

- Many U.S. companies failed due to fraud, poor management, and/or the management betting wrongly. When the CEO is using the company as his own AMT, or having an extravagant life style, watch out. If they promise you a return doubling the current rate of return of the market, listen to your wise mother: there is no free lunch. Despite so many real examples, still fools are born every day, because greed is a human nature.

- Do not follow the 'commentators' on TV. They have their own hidden agenda which usually is not in your interest.

- Many companies fail due to their lack of ability to pay back their loans. Except for specific industries and situations, avoid companies with high debt (Debt/Equity over 50%). Financial institutions and companies that have high debt in order to finance their products for their customers such as utilities are the exceptions.

- I have a screen named Big Losers beating the market by more than 600% in Early Recovery (a phase defined by me). However, some bankrupted companies are not included in the database which is termed as survivor bias. Hence, the actual result is far worse than the 600%. I still use this screen but skip these companies using the following yardsticks.
    - The companies are usually safe with high Free Cash Flow / Equity and high Expected Profit / Stock Price.
    - The following are red flags: low Free Cash Flow / Equity, high Inventory and high Receivable (esp. relative to its Payable), high P/B (over 30) and high net Debt/Equity (over 1 to 3 depending on the industry).
    - P/PFC should be greater than 0 and less than 50. A healthy cash flow may not be able to service the debt if it is too huge. Hence, compare it to Debt/Equity. Compare the cash flow per year to debt obligations per year.

- New government regulations could bankrupt an industry. What would happen when the U.S. takes out the rebates and subsidies of solar panels? When the U.S. banned solar panels from China, one of my Chinese stocks went bankrupt. Also government bailed out bankrupting companies such as Chrysler (that I made a good profit) and AIG Fannie Mae in 2008.
- Serious lawsuits- Most U.S. companies are required to file this information in their financial reports.
- Obsolete products. Newspapers, retail and similar products would be replaced by the internet. The opposite is new products such as virtual reality products.
- Many companies run out of money during the development phase of the major products. Many are too optimistic in their business plans.
- If you expect the market will recover in 2 years, ensure the company's cash and net income can support their burn rate for at least two more years.
- Many investing sites (most require subscriptions) have safety scores.
- If the Beneish M-Score is greater than -2.22, the company is likely an accounting manipulator.
- Choose companies with Z-Score higher than 3; it does not applicable to financial companies. Both M-Score and Z-Score are available from GuruFocus, a paid subscription. Z-Score does not work for financial institutions.
- Z-Score metrics are: "Working Capital / Total Assets" (A), "Retained Earnings / Total Assets" (B), "Earnings Before Interest & Taxes / Total Assets" (C), "Market Cap / Total Liabilities" (D) and "Sales / Total Assets" (E).
  Z-Score = 1.2 A + 1.4 B + 3.3 C +.6 D + E
- Market timing- It does not always work, but it is far better to follow a proven technique than not. It is far safer to take money out of the market when the market is too risky or is plunging. The big losers are companies that provide non-essential products in a down turn.
- Small companies could be risky but very profitable. Typically they have a low stock price (less than $5), small market cap (less than 50 M), low sales (less than $25 M) and low institutional ownership (less than 5%).
- Avoid companies when their own bond ratings are not equal to AAA or AA (www.moodys.com).

8   When to sell a stock

There are many reasons to sell a stock as follows.

Personal

1. Has met my targets/objectives.
    It could be a 10% gain in a very short-term swing, x% return in 4 months for a short-term swing or y% gain after a year for long-term trades. Define x and y depending on your risk tolerance and how often you trade.

    I bought 4 stocks in one day during the August, 2015 correction and placed sell orders with 10% more than my purchase prices. I sold one in a day and another one within a month. This is my strategy for correction – sometimes it works and sometimes it does not.

    Never look back. Do not blame yourself when the prices are better than your trade prices. When the market is volatile, use a higher percent of the current prices. Be disciplined. Stay on the same strategy and detach yourself from emotions.

2. Realize that we have made a mistake. Do not let your ego block your eyes. It could be due to bad analysis, bad, data, unexpected fraud, lawsuits, and/or unforeseeable events that you have no control of. It is better to get out with a small loss. I prefer a 25% loss as a threshold for long-term strategies and a 10% (or less for some strategies) loss for short-term strategies.

    We have to ensure whether it is a mistake or not. If the 'mistake' is just bad luck or due to conditions we cannot possibly predict or control, then it is not a mistake. If it is a mistake, learn from it. When we diversify, one bad loss should not cause a big dent in our portfolios. The stop loss is a good tool most of the time except when there is a flash crash.

    If the criteria have been faithfully followed and it does not work well, check out whether your criteria are wrong, or it does not work on the current market conditions.

3. When we have too many stocks in the same sector, we will want to replace some stocks to better diversify our portfolios.

   When the sector is rising, we want to weigh more on that sector at the expense of diversification, and vice versa. Set a limit of how many sectors you should hold.

4. Need cash for living expenses.

5. To reduce a tax burden by selling some losers. Tax consideration should not be the primary reason for selling. Take advantage of the favorable tax treatment for long-term capital gains. In short, sell losers within the short term limit (currently a year), and sell winners after 365 days; check the current tax laws.

   Harvest tax losses. Sell losers and buy back similar stocks (or same stock after 31 days to avoid wash sale). It is not too clear in which you can buy back the same loser in your children's account under the current tax law.

6. To take advantage of a lower tax. In 2013, we can pay virtually zero (except the increase of tax on social security payment) Federal income taxes on long-term capital gains when our income is below a specific tax bracket (15% as of 2015). Check out the current tax laws. Evaluate the sold winners for a possible buy back.

Market Timing

7. When the market or the sector plunges, sell stocks or stocks within the sector.

   For temporary peaks, evaluate which stocks in your portfolio to sell based on fundamentals. The objective is to raise cash for buying opportunities.

Deteriorating appreciation potential

8. There may be some stocks that have a better appreciation potential than the ones you currently own. Churning the portfolio by replacing better stocks may cost some brokerage commissions (some are free today) and taxes for taxable

accounts, but it improves the quality and the appreciation potential for the entire portfolio.

9. The company's fundamentals have changed for the worse. If you use a scoring system, compare the current score with the score you actually bought the stock for. Apple is a good example from 2013 to 2015. Buy when the fundamentals are good and sell when they are not.

   The basic fundamentals are expected P/E, the quarter-to-quarter earnings growth rate / the sales growth rate, and Debt /Equity.

   When your stocks have passed the peak and started to decline, sell them. When they are heading to bankruptcy, sell them fast.

Hints that the fundamentals are degrading

Evaluate the stocks you own at least every 6 months and check their daily news at least once a week that can be easily done using Seeking Alpha's portfolio function.

- The cash flow is decreasing fast. Cash flow is not a particularly good predicative indicator for appreciation, but a good indicator on whether the company will survive. This metric is very hard to manipulate.

- A new or pending lawsuit. Check out how serious the lawsuit is and be aware that a minor lawsuit can be ignored. Companies always sue against each other.

- A big drop in sales. Do not be alarmed when a new product, or a new drug is going to replace a major product. Compare sales to the same quarter of prior year to avoid seasonal fluctuations (Q-to-Q info I available from Finviz.com).

- Management deteriorates- One hint is the deteriorating ROE from the last quarter.

- The extravagant life style of the CEO and the many easy loans to officers.

- Poor operations. They include recalls of products such as the GM recall on ignition switches, product secrets being stolen and customers' credit card info being stolen. Boeing's 747-Max is a warning call.

- A successful product from the competitor, or the current product is losing its market share, or becoming a low-profit commodity.

- Insiders and/or institutional investors are dumping the companies' stocks far more than the averages (2% for me) especially in heavy volumes and by more than one insider.

  o Have more than one insider dumping a lot of the stock within a month and no insider purchase in that month.

  o Have more than one insider decrease their holdings by more than 10%.

- When the SEC or any government agency pays attention to a company, it usually means bad news.

- Deceptive accounting practices have been discovered.

- Increasing receivable and/or inventory at an alarming rate.

- Earnings have been restated too many times.

- Short percentage is increasing fast – someone found something wrong with the company.

- The invalidity of 'one-time charges'.

- Abnormal return rate of the company's pension fund comparing to the average of the companies in the same sector.

- Too many and too costly reconstructing charges.

- The entire stock market is plunging as indicated by our chart in detecting market crashes.

- The stock price does not move up with good news. It shows the price has peaked.

- The accumulation amount is far less than the sold amount. When the stock price is up, the accumulation is less than the sold stocks when the stock price was down the last time. It indicates that no more accumulation is ahead and hence the stock will be down most likely.

Afterthoughts

- Another article on this topic.
  http://buzz.money.cnn.com/2013/04/05/stocks-sell/
  An article from Investopedia. Nothing new but it is worth having the same second opinion.
  http://www.investopedia.com/financial-edge/0412/5-tips-on-when-to-sell-your-stock.aspx

- It also depends on your strategies. I sell most of my stocks in my momentum portfolio within a month. At least one strategy I know of does not keep any stock during the peak stage of the market cycle – the easiest time to make money but also the riskiest time.

  If you use charts for trading, sell the stocks that are below your moving averages or other technical analysis indicators. Personally I do not use charts for making sell decisions due to my limited time.

- Sell when the company is heading into bankruptcy as described before. The red flags are: 1. Negative cash flow. 2. Heavy insiders dumping the stocks. 3. Pending major lawsuit. 4. Fraud from the management.
- Risky periods for a stock.
  Earnings announcement (4 times a year), settling a major lawsuit and/or during a FDA event in approving a drug are risky periods for a stock. A fluctuation more than 5% in either direction is normal. Some use options to buy insurance. Most ignore it. For the majority of the time, heavy insider purchase is a good indicator. There are rumors (or educated guesses) on earnings before their announcements. Zacks is supposed to be a good subscription for earnings estimates.

Section VI: Strategies

You may want to paper trade each screen. Select the one that is favorable to the current market (i.e. it performs best in the last three months). In addition, it has to fit your risk tolerance and your own requirements. In addition, different phases of the market cycle favor specific sectors and investing strategies. For example, the market bottom stage favors value stocks while the market up stage

1   Introduction

A strategy is a method or a procedure in how to find stocks (usually via screens, also known as searches), analyze the stocks, buy them and sell them. This section concentrates on screening for stocks.

I prefer value stocks (i.e. based on fundamentals). However, fundamentals are secondary for some strategies such as momentum. This book uses the same techniques in Finding Stocks and Scoring Stocks, so they will not be repeated here.

This book describes some simpler strategies and leaves the complicated ones in their own books that follow.

I read the book "What Works on Wall Street" by James O'Shaughnessy blaming many other strategies for non-performance. Later I read another book mentioning that O'Shaughnessy did not work after he published his book.

As mentioned previously, the strategy will not be effective when there are too many followers. That's the reason I provide you with many strategies and you should explore newer strategies yourself. The market favors different groups of strategies in different stages of the market cycle.

The best way to check what is the favorable strategy is to test the performances of your different strategies for the last three to six months. Several low-cost subscription services provide a historical database to make this task simple and feasible.

Traders and hedge fund managers change their strategies frequently. Retail investors should do the same.

One strategy was the poster boy for a subscription service. It worked well before. I tested it recently and it was one of the worst strategies. The lesson is: There are no evergreen strategies. Test out whether they still work in the last 90 days.

A Sample Strategy

It is an example. Adjust it to your preferences and requirements. Instead of buying stocks, just save them in a watch list and buy them when the entire market is on sale. It consists of the following three steps.

1. When to search stocks to be traded. For example, it is once a month when the market is not risky.
2. What to buy. It will be described in more detail later.
3. Sell the stock(s). When the market is plunging, your objectives have been satisfied, or the bought stock(s) does not satisfy most criteria described in #2.

Step #2. There are several steps: Fundamental Analysis, Intangible Analysis, Qualitative Analysis and Technical Analysis.

For simplicity, stick with Fundamental Analysis here. The stocks have to satisfy most of the following criteria. Try to use a screener to limit your selection. If you do not find any stock, relax the criteria or do nothing as the market may be peaking and/or expensive. Skip those criteria that you do not have a subscription to access to.

- It must be in one of the three major U.S. exchanges. No ADRs and partnerships (unless you're an expert in the countries/fields).
- Market Cap is over 100 M (or over 10B for blue chips).
- Price is over $2.
- Average daily volume must be at least 20 times more than your potential position.
- Expected P/E is less than 20 and E must be positive.
- P/Cash Flow is less than 25 and Cash Flow must be positive.
- Debt/Equity is less than 1 (preferable .5; also depending on specific industry).
- Fidelity's Analyst Opinion is 7 or higher.

2 Experiences in strategies

A strategy tells you what stocks to buy, what and when to sell.

We should use one or a few of the proven strategies that match well with the current market conditions. It is not an easy job and not an exact science especially when human emotions are involved. A perfect match seldom happens. However, when it does, it can be fireworks and your pocket will be over-stuffed with money.

The following strategies are for illustration purposes only. Test them out before you use them with real money.

- We usually ignore when to sell. If the strategy such as the "Year-End Loser" shows statistically that the best holding period is 4 months, sell them before May. That's why we should have the performances at short-term, mid-term and long-term in testing strategies.

- Sideways market (such as 2015).

   Buy at dips and sell at temporary highs and vice versa. It is a correction about 5% by my definition. The market may just fluctuate in a small range.

   The hard part is to determine what these dips and bottoms are. Here are my suggestions and how we need to adjust the percentages to the volatility of the current market. To me, if it is 2% lower than the last session (or 5% lower than the highest price in the last 5 sessions), it is a temporary bottom. The definitions vary based on your personal tolerance and time for investing. To benefit in this small fluctuation, buy stocks from your watch list or any ETF that represents the market such as SPY or IWM.

   The holding period could be one day to two weeks depending on your risk tolerance. It takes advantage of the fluctuation of prices due to the good news and bad news scenario typically.

   Alternatively, you determine when to sell by how much it would rise such as 2% higher than the last session (or 5% higher than the lowest price in the last 5 sessions). The disadvantage is you may never be able to sell stocks that are continuously heading down. The stop orders would prevent further losses.

In reality, the market does not behave the way we expected it to. You need to protect your loss (say sell it when it is over 15% loss). In the long run and if the market fits this sideways market, you SHOULD make money. As in life, there are no guarantees. You can load the historical price of SPY (or another ETF) to stimulate this strategy using different percentages and holding periods.

- The market is up or down steadily.

  Strategies using momentum profit better than buying value stocks in a bull market. "Buy high and sell higher" is a good strategy in a rising market.

  Use contra ETFs on a down ward market. The average holding period for me is 1 month (some may use 3 months). I stop using momentum when the market is too risky as I do not usually short stocks. It takes several weeks of small profits to recover from one big loss in one day that is if it recovers.

- Buy value.

  The average holding period could be more than one year. You're betting against the tide, so it will take a longer time for the value to be 'discovered' by the market. When the institution retailers are selling, find out their reasons. Buy what they are selling if they are wrong (rarely but it has happened many times). It is similar to "Buy low and sell high" and "Contrary Strategy". It seems to be easier said than done, as our emotions do not allow us to act rationally. The typical retail investor usually buys at peaks and sells at bottoms.

- Turnaround and breakup of a company.

  When the company fixes its major problem(s), its stock price could skyrocket.

A company may be worth more by adding up the pieces. The recent example is ALU when I bought it at $1 in 2013. At the time, the company had a market cap of around two billions but the debt is about the same. However, their patents could be worth far more than two billion.

- Follow talented investors.

  First, you need to find the talented investors who have good recent performance records. GuruFocus.com (subscription is required) shows what stocks the gurus recently traded. 2015 is not a good year for gurus.

  Check out this article.
  http://seekingalpha.com/article/2762935-a-wisdom-of-experts-portfolio

- Follow what insiders buy.
  There are many tricks to separate the gems from garbage.

- Buy at the bottoms.
  2009 is one bottom. In my definition, it is Early Recovery (usually about one year from the plunge or indicated by the chart described in this book). This bottom fishing strategy buys beaten down stocks that are fundamentally sound. The average holding time is about one year (less if there are better bargains).

  My best returns are from the last two bottoms in 2003 and 2009. At these times, there were more potential stocks for huge profits and my average holding period was about 6 months. 2009 was the only time I dipped into my credit line on my house - **not recommended to most investors**.

- Market Neutral.
  If you are a good stock picker (or believe you're one), treat the market as neutral (i.e. ignoring the market timing). For example, you pick five stocks to buy and five stocks to sell short. You make money due to your skill in picking the right stocks no matter how the market moves. In theory, you should make good money without betting on the market direction.

- Sector Neutral.

If you specialize in a specific sector such as airlines, you may buy 2 good stocks and short 2 bad stocks in that sector. You can make good money because of your knowledge in the sector. In this strategy, compare stocks to its sector averages. You can use options to do the same if your cash position is limited.

Trading drug stocks could bring you huge profits. To improve your odds, you need to be an expert in this field. If you're not, subscribe to a specific newsletter that specializes in this industry and has a proven track record. Weigh more on the buy side when the sector is heading up, and vice versa.

- Sector Rotation.
  Investing in a sector or shorting the entire sector could add more profit. To illustrate, the tech sector may be a laggard during a recession as most consumers will not have the spare money to buy consumer electronics, and many companies would postpone their investment in enhancing productivity and development. Every month or two, rotate to the sector that is in an uptrend. Protect your profit when the sector reverses its direction.

- Theme investing.
  When China is moving up, FXI (an ETF) would be a buy. Other examples are OIL and GLD (for gold).

- Strong USD.
  It would be bad for global companies when the profits from foreign investments would be reduced when they are converted to a strong USD. The other bet is on USD itself.

- Super stocks.
  Most are small companies with increasing sales and earnings. It is a little different from the conventional stock analysis. They are riskier but the profits could be huge. Expect one big winner for several small losers. These stocks of small companies are not followed by analysts.

- The winners are already in your portfolio.
  Do not sell your winners as they may turn into bigger winners unless you have a good reason. Do not sell them if they still pass your recent stock analysis. During any market plunge, you may

want to sell them but you should buy them back when the market recovers.

When you mismatch the strategy with the market conditions, you lose the opportunity for profit or even lose money. If the market is up or down steadily, a sideways strategy will not work for example. Matching the strategy to the current market conditions is not an easy job and sometimes it takes some luck. However, when it matches it, there could be fireworks. If you match it more times than you miss it, you should make good money.

Afterthoughts

"Buy and hold" needs no explanation. You just buy the stock and hold it forever. It is a good strategy in a secular bull market such as 1970-2000. After 2000, there are better strategies than "Buy and Hold".

A better way is "Buy and monitor" to ensure the stock you bought still has an appreciation potential.

"Buy and forget" is my term and it could be a good strategy in 2012. Buy the deeply-valued stocks (i.e. big bargains for quality stocks) and forget it until the economy comes back. I have made some profits in established companies such as MSFT, CAT and CSCO during this period.

Links
Market Neutral http://en.wikipedia.org/wiki/Market_neutral
Sector Rotation http://en.wikipedia.org/wiki/Sector_rotation

3   Strategy performance

We may find some strategies performing well in testing but not in reality. Here are my possible explanations.

- Survival bias. When Lehman Brothers and other bankrupt financial institutions are taken out from your historical database, your strategy would look better. Try not to include penny stocks and stocks with micro market caps as they have a higher chance of going bankrupt. Mergers and acquisition do not offset this effect as they are fewer.

- Test windows. For example, start each test with the start of the month and end the test a year later. If the testing period is 5 years, you should have 5*12 = 60 tests. When you start with an amount and let it rise and fall for a long period, the final result would be affected greatly on how it performed in the first year. Most advertised tests are not reliable as they always cherry pick a date that is profitable in the starting years of the test.

- Test different holding periods such as 3 (1 for momentum strategies), 6 and 12 months. Some strategies are good for a short-term hold.

- The last 5 years is better than the last 10 years as it is more similar to the recent market.

- Define your tests according to the phases of the market cycle. Market Peak (a phase defined by me) should have different strategies than Early Recovery.

- Compare the performance to SPY (or an ETF that simulates the market). If most of the stocks you trade are small stocks, use an ETF for small stocks.

- Consider dividends in some cases where they are applicable. For example, for a flat market, the average 1.5% dividend makes a huge difference.

- Use annualized returns. They are better for comparison. However, the returns of less than a month should not be considered as they amplify the results too much.

- Ensure the calculations are correct. When you compare the returns to SPY, the negative values could give wrong interpretations.
- My broker calculates my performance returns and compares them to the indexes. It is handy.

  I gifted appreciated stocks to my son. My broker did it wrong in calculating performance (but correctly for tax purposes) by using the original cost basis. Hence they look far better than they actually are.
- Data fitting works sometimes but not all the time. You change the parameters to boost the best performance. Sometimes it does not work due to the market conditions that are not the same and/or your data is too small to reach a useful conclusion.

4   Different investment styles

There are three major styles to evaluate stocks: Fundamental, Growth and Technical Analysis (TA).

The debate on their benefits could be endless. I believe TA is good for short term (1 month for stocks), growth for intermediate term (say 3 months) and fundamental is good for longer term (say 6 months). Here is my summary of the two (I place Fundamental and Growth into the same group for discussion here).   Market sometimes favors value (i.e. fundamentals) and sometimes growth.

TA depends mostly on the stock price and hence it predicts the trend better; it also can track oversold conditions. TA would catch the stock movement, but not by fundamental or growth metrics.

- TA.
  Most TAers do not care about fundamentals, but price and volume. They do have good arguments. A lot of data about the stock are not available or too late to be effective such as a new drug discovery, being acquired, or a serious lawsuit pending.

  The following are two illustrations on how TAers can benefit.

  When the insiders and/or analysts know about some promising new products or positive unexpected earnings, they buy and tell their families to buy. I do not judge whether it is Illegal insider trading or not. TAers notice the rise of the stock price with increasing volume and they buy. Many times the last ones to buy may end up losing money as the insiders would unload them especially when the stock prices are over-valued.

  When the institutional investors (pension fund managers and fund managers) are buying a specific stock, the stock volume and its price will both rise. TAers would notice them from the charts and jump on the wagon. To me, this is the basic reason on how good day traders make money. It usually takes a week for an institutional investor to finish trading a stock.

- Fundamentals.
  They look at the companies' metrics such as P/E, expected P/E, PEG, debt, sales growth, etc. A good company's stock price with

rising profit and rising sales should appreciate in the long term. Some short the stocks of companies with bad fundamentals. In some cases, data is hidden in the financial statements that most metrics do not detect.

To conclude, the best TAers and the best fundamentalists usually make money in either market in the long run. However, fundamental analysis is easier to master and they have made more money than TAers in the long run. You find a lot of successful fundamentalists from Buffett and his followers, but not too many successful TAers. Some successful TAers even lose their accumulated fortunes. Be warned that if you do not know what you're doing in either discipline, you will lose money. Learn it and trade it on paper before committing even small amounts of real money to it.

The best way is use both disciplines in selecting stocks as described below.

- When your chart(s) displays a candidate to buy, take a look at the fundamentals. If the fundamentals are bad, be cautious. Some screens can search for the stocks with good technical patterns (Finviz.com is one).

- After you spot a bargain stock to buy via the fundamental metrics, check out its SMA-200 (Simple Moving Average for the last 200 trade sessions) or any duration that fits your purpose. If the price is above the moving average, it could be a buy.

Afterthoughts

- Try the following to see whether fundamental works better if you have a historical database.

  Fundamentals

  1. Include all stocks that are below the 200-day SMA (Simple Moving Average) - opposite of what a TAer would do.
  2. The expected positive P/Es have to be between 4 and 15. In addition, both profits and sales are rising by 5%.

3. Exclude financial companies like banks and insurance, miners, bio companies and drug companies that are hard to evaluate.

TA

1. Buy stocks that cross over the 50-day, simple moving averages.
2. Never buy stocks when the market is below 200-day, simple moving average.

Check the result in 1 month intervals and 6 months intervals. My own simple test favors the fundamentals in 6 months intervals and favors TA in 1 month intervals. You may need more exhaustive testing to draw a good conclusion in different phases of a market cycle for at least 2 market cycles.

- SMA-200 (from Finviz.com without charts) and its variations are the ones most TAers use and even most experienced fundamentalists know how to use it if they want to. It is also a good indicator for the general market by using an ETF that simulates the market.
  There are many sophisticated TA indicators in Yahoo!Finance. For qualified clients, Fidelity provides a tool to back test your TA strategies.

- It may be beneficial to use fundamentals to look for stocks and use TA to find the entry and exit points. Today's screens can do it in the reverse order, or both in the same screen.

- Fundamental can be divided into Value and Growth.
  Value. I use it mostly. Especially good in early recovery phase of the market cycle.

5   AAII, a source for strategies

AAII has many nice stock screens. Check out their performance summaries. You can divide the screens and their performances into groups according to the different stages of a market cycle and rank the performances. Some screens perform better in certain stage(s) of the market cycle. Most likely, the value screens should do better in market bottom (Early Recovery defined by me) and growth screens do better in a bull market (Up and Peak phases defined by me).

As a regular subscriber, the screen stock recommendations are about 15 days old (check the current policy) and the most updated screens require extra cost. Their strategy for most screens is: Sell all stocks that do not meet the criteria of the screen and buy new stocks that meet the criteria every month. This trading strategy would require a lot of trades and you need to consider their tax consequences (none for non-taxable accounts) and commissions. Trade on paper before you commit to their recommendations with real money similar to many strategies described in this book.

The basic membership with a decent magazine-publication is a good deal. If you are new to investing, there are many basic books provided on their web site.

Update 2/2016

AAII publishes its screen performance every year. Here are some pointers.

- Do not follow last year's winners. I predicted 2015 was a sideways market and 2016 is a risky market that has a good chance to turn into a bear market.
- During bear markets, the screens had lost from 10% to 83% without a single winner here. When the technical indicator SMA-350 or Death Cross tells you to exit, exit as there is no screen that would find winners.
- Every year from 2011 to 2015, the return of the market is positive after adding dividends. When the technical indicator SMA-350 or Death Cross tells you to invest, invest if you trust the charts.

- Some screens work great in one year and become big losers in another year. To conclude, there is no evergreen screen.
- It does not go earlier than 2009 in the summaries, the last Early Recovery that has the best profit potential. I recommend value stocks for this stage of the market cycle.
- For the same reason above, it does not show performances in the bear market of 2007-2008.
- I would select the screens that have a good five year average. However, the last five years is a typical bull market. Most screens do not beat the S&P500's 12% average for the last five years. You're better off buying SPY, an ETF simulating the S&P 500 index.
- AAII screens have high turnovers as they replace the stocks when they do not meet the screen criteria.

Paper art by Eric from PowPaper

6   *The best strategy*

Note. Most parameters described here such as SMA-20% and Short% can be found from Finviz.com

It is Buy Low and Sell High.

It is simple but most retail investors just do the opposite: Buy High and Sell Low. The flow of money to/from money market funds turns out to be a reliable contrary indicator.

The Early Recovery in 2003 and 2009 and the later part of June, 2012 could be the best time to buy.

The above represents buying at low prices and selling at high prices. Considering P/E (positive 'E' only), buy at low P/E of a stock, a sector and the market (via an ETF) and sell them respectively at high P/E.

Here are some hints when to buy and sell with this strategy:

- Sell when everyone including your silly mother-in-law is making good money and all participants think they're financial geniuses. It could be the riskiest time. The high interest rates (my yardstick is over 5% for Fed Discount rate, the best rate the Fed lends to the banks) usually confirms this as folks falsely expect better returns even though they pay more on interest to borrow money to buy stocks.

- Do not buy the stocks that were the bubble-forming stocks such as the technology stocks in 2001-2002 and the bank stocks in 2008-2009 as some 'optimists' think it is time to return and usually they're wrong.

  Do not think the stock is a good deal when it loses half of its value. Buy them only when the root problem has been fixed. The best time to return to the market after a market plunge is usually two years after the market plunge (2003 for the market plunge in 2000 and 2009 for the market plunge in 2007/2008). Many bubble stocks never recover and many of these stocks take more than 3 years to recover. Their prices appear to be low, but no one can predict the bottom unless it goes to zero.

- Be careful in the sectors or group of stocks that have a winning streak for more than two years. Most likely they will correct. Use a stop loss to protect your profits if you want to keep them.

  You could have saved a lot if you used this strategy on tech stocks in 2000. As of 2015, dividend stocks could be the next sector to burst, but only time can tell. Do not fall in love with a stock. Yesterday's winners could be tomorrow's losers, and vice versa.

  'Buy and hold' has been dead since 2000. We have two market plunges with an average loss of about 45% from their peaks.

- Do not buy dividend stocks solely for their dividends. Most of them are matured companies; most have less growth and hence less appreciation potential. They usually lose less value in a recession after dividends. Income investors are chasing them for higher dividends than bonds.

  Except from Roth accounts, when you withdraw from your retirement accounts, your dividends will be treated as income. Check the current tax rates for income and dividend from taxable accounts.

- Buy value stocks that seem to be bottomed. It is hard to identify the bottom. When the appreciation potential outweighs the risk, it could be a buy.

- No one can predict consistently the market bottom. However, use your better judgment with educated guesses to gain an edge. Refer to the exit point using the 350-day SMA from the chapter on detecting market plunges.

- Buy the stocks that have been losing money but their burn rates can last for the entire recession. They're risky but the potential profits are great. There were many in 2003 and 2009. Even in a bad economy in 2012, a few corporations had historically low P/Es.

- Buy value stocks with a turnaround sign such as when the SMA-50% is positive.

- Buy against the experts who have unconvincing predictions. They usually exaggerate the rosy outlooks of the companies in order to sell the stocks they own. This is one of the few times you should bet against them. Use your better judgment to ensure how false their predications could be.

Using Citicorp (symbol C) as an example

Following the chapter on avoiding bank stocks, buying this stock at $550 a share could be avoided. After the big plunge in 2008, I believe it has long-term profit potential. Accumulate this stock if you believe C will be profitable in 10 years (2024) or so. Do not sell it unless there is potential for a market plunge. If so, buy it back after the plunge. One's opinion.

With our market timing (defending sector may return in two years), I checked it in mid 2009, about 2 years after the start of the market plunge. Optionally I could use the SMA-350 of the stock to determine the reentry point. However, it had no meaning due to the big plunge from $550. On 8/2009, C's P/E was negative, so I did not buy it.

Alternatively buy it for when there is a big drop in P/E regardless of the current price as follows. We started when the P/E is about 40. Normally I buy it when the P/E is at around 20. Take an exception for turnaround stocks.

Date	P/E	Price
06/2010	40	40
01/2011	13	49
08/2011	9	32

The above is for illustration purposes only, so the numbers are not precise.

As of 6/12/2014, I expected a correction, so I sold it at about $48. I only trade this kind of stocks when I see long-term appreciation potential. The other three important metrics are P/B, P/S and RSI(14). Use Forward (same as Expected) P/E if possible. The most important metric for lenders is the quality of the loans, which is hard to evaluate for retail investors. The other factor is any serious, pending lawsuits. When Lehman Brothers was gone, the governments will chase after the institutions that sold the derivatives.

Update 8/2019. C's stock price is $62.

The second best strategy

Buy high and sell higher.

When everyone is looking for stocks with the highest value, there may not be any such stocks available. It seems to contradict with my best strategy but it is not intended to. Fundamentals may not show everything about the company such as a new drug, a new product... The all-time high prices usually show that. Buy the stock when it is over the 50-day simple moving average (50 or 200 days depending on how long you usually hold a stock) via Finviz.com.

Buying fully-priced stocks is dangerous even if it may be profitable. To protect your profits:

- Be extra careful in risky market; I prefer not to buy any stock when the market is risky.

- Set stop loss orders. Recommend 10% (or 15% for volatile stocks) less than the current price. If you set a 5% stop, it would be stopped out by normal fluctuations especially for volatile stocks.

- Use Technical Analysis. When the price drops below the moving average you used, sell it. When RSI (14) is high (over 70), check out the reason as it could be overbought.

If you are not very sure, sell half of it. You will not go broke for taking profits.

As in life, there are no guarantees, but using a proven technique / discipline is far better than trading without one. Paper trading ensures the strategy fits the current market conditions, your personal tolerance and requirements.

The third best strategy

Buy very high and sell even higher.

It is the riskiest. These stocks could be bubble stocks moved by institutional investors and then moved even higher by retail investors. It may take a while before the institutional investors rotate to another sector / stocks and/or take profit.

My strategy is to follow the herd but ensure you're ready to exit.

- Find them. Usually they have break-outs. They pass the resistance, a technical term. Now, they are in the low point of the support line, so they have a long way to go to the next resistance line. It has to be confirmed with its daily volume such as 3 times or more than the average daily volume. Usually they are in the 52-week highs.

- Usually they are large caps with high trade volumes. My range is 100M to 5B. Be careful on stocks ranging from 100M to 500M. They may appreciate a lot on the positive side; they are risky and they can be manipulated easier. Stocks from 1B to 5B appreciation potential is lesser than 100M to 500M.

- Do not short them.

- Buy them ignoring the fundamentals as they are moving up with the herd sometimes for a reason and sometimes not. Alternatively, use options.

- Set mental stop losses. Adjust the stops periodically after they have been appreciated.

  Watch them every day. Bring up Finviz.com and enter the sector ETF the stock belongs to and the stocks. Pay attention to SMA200%: The higher it is, the higher chance it is peaking. When RSI(14) is over 70% (65% for sectors), most likely it is overbought. When SMA-20% is negative, there is a good chance of reversing the trend downward.

Buy and Monitor

I usually sell my stocks that have fulfilled my objectives or admitted I have made a mistake. However, some stocks keep on rising and I may miss many 3 or more baggers.

I gifted many appreciated stocks to my family members. My grandchildren will keep them for a long while. Here are the stocks I gave on 5/1/2015 (the date I gifted them) and the performances today (5/12/2018).

Stock	Total Return	Annualized return
CSCO	58%	19%
STX	88%	29%
TTWO	377%	124%
Average	174%	57%
Compare to:		
SPY	29%	10%

My point is "buy and hold" is still valid for many stocks. Buy low when they have been temporarily ignored. These stocks should have long-term potential as they will be held for a long while. My actual performance is substantially more as I bet at least double more in TTWO.

Instead of "Buy and Hold", you need buy and monitor. When they have serious problems such as Circuit City, Radio Shack, Sears…, do not hesitate to sell them.

When you time the market, ensure buy back the stocks you sold during the recovery phase of the market cycle.

My long-term grade

They are composed of the following (using metrics from Finviz.com): low Forward P/E, low Debt/Eq, Cash/sh, larger Market Cap, ROE, low RSI(14), Insider Own, Sales Q/Q, EPS Q/Q, SMA200… In addition, they have good products for the future and they invest heavily in research.

7   Miscellaneous strategies

A strategy tells you what stocks to buy, what and when to sell.

We should use one of the proven strategies that match well with the current market conditions. It is not an easy job and not an exact science especially when human emotions are involved. A perfect match seldom happens. However, when it does or it is close, it will be firework and your pocket will be over-stuffed with dollar bills.

The following strategies are for illustration only. Test them out before you use them with real money.

- Side way market (such as during March to July 2012).

    Buy at dips and sell at temporary highs and vice versa. It is a correction less than 5% by my definition. The market just fluctuates in a small range.

    The hard part is to determine what these dips and bottoms are. Here are my suggestions and we need to adjust the percentages to the volatility of the current market. To me, if it is 2% lower than the last session (or 5% lower than the highest price in the last 5 sessions), it is a temporary bottom. To benefit this small fluctuation, buy any ETF that represents the market such as SPY or IWM.

    The holding period could be one day to two weeks depending on your risk tolerance. It takes advantage of the fluctuation of prices due to good news and bad news scenario.

    Alternatively, you determine when to sell buy by how much it would rise such as 2% higher than the last session (or 5% higher than the lowest price in the last 5 sessions).

    I have assumed the best scenario (i.e. always making money). In reality, the market does not behave the way we expect. To protect our loss, you need to protect your loss (say sell it when it is over 5% loss). In the long run and if the market fits this side way market, you SHOULD make money. As in life, there is no guarantee. You can load the historical price of SPY (or other ETFs) to simulate this strategy using different percentages and holding periods.

The market from April to July, 2013 could be volatile with our debt problems re-surfacing and solutions being 'identified' and the news on EU crisis.

- The market is up or down steadily.

Strategies using momentum profit better than buying value stocks in a bull market. Buy high and sell higher in a rising market.

Use contra ETFs on a down market. The average holding period for me is 1 month to me (some use 3 months). I stop using momentum when the market is risky. It takes several weeks of small profits to recover one big loss in one day.

- Buy value.

The average holding period could be more than one year. You're betting against the tide, so it will take longer time for the value to be 'discovered' by the market. When the institution retailers are selling, find out their reasons. Eat their lunches by buying what they are selling if they are manipulating the market. Buy low and sell high. It seems to be easily said than done, as our emotion does not allow us to act rationally. The typical retail investor usually buys at peaks and sells at bottoms. It turns into 'Buy high and sell low' and it is the worst.

- Turnaround and breakup of a company.

When the company fixes its major problem, its stock price could skyrocket.

A company may worth more by adding up the pieces. The recent example is ALU when I bought it at $1 in 2013. At the time, the company had a market cap of around two billions but the debt is about the same. However, their patents could worth for two billions.

- Follow talented investors.

First, you need to find the talented investors who have good recent performance records. GuruFocus.com (subscription required) shows what stocks the gurus recently traded.

- Follow what insiders buy.
  There are many tricks to separate the gems from garbage. I have a brief description in a separate chapter.

- Buy at bottoms.
  2009 is one bottom. In my definition, it is Early Recovery (usually about one year from the plunge or indicated by the chart described in this book). This bottom fishing strategy buys beaten stocks that are fundamentally sound. The average holding time is about one year (less if there are better bargains) and the average one year return from the bottom is greater than 25% for me.

  My best returns are from the last two bottoms in 2003 and 2009. At these times, there were more potential stocks for huge profits and my average holding period was about 6 months. 2009 was the only time I dipped into my credit line on my house - not recommended to most investors.

- Market Neutral.
  If you are a good stock picker (or believe you're one), treat the market as neutral (i.e. ignoring market timing). For example, you pick five stocks to buy and five stocks to sell short. You make money due to your skill in picking the right stocks no matter how the market moves. In theory, you should make good money without betting on the market direction. However, theory seldom resembles reality and the market is not always rational.

- Sector Neutral.
  If you specialize in a specific sector such as airlines, you buy 2 good stocks and short 2 bad stocks in that sector for example. You make money because of your knowledge in the sector. In this strategy, compare stocks to its sector averages. You can use options to do the same if your cash position is limited.
  Trading drug stocks could bring huge profits. To improve your odds, you need to be an expert in this field. If you're not, subscribe a specific newsletter that specializes in this industry and has a proven record.

- Sector Rotation.
  Investing in a sector or shorting the entire sector could add more profit. To illustrate, the tech sector may be a laggard during a recession as most consumers will not have the spare money to buy consumer electronics and many companies would postpone their investment in enhancing productivity and development.

- All is better than one.
  You can follow the successful stock pickers such as Buffett. Do not follow the past heroes. Many screens simulate what the experts would buy and they are available from many free sites or from your broker. GuruFocus.com provides an updated list of stocks picked by the gurus. Check out this article.

  http://seekingalpha.com/article/2762935-a-wisdom-of-experts-portfolio

- Super stocks.
  Most are small companies with increasing sales and earnings. It is a little different from the conventional stock analysis. They are riskier but the profits could be huge. Expect one big winner for several small losers. I have written a book titled SuperStocks.

- Buy winners in Nov. as fund managers buy them to dress up their fund offerings and sell losers in Dec. as retail investors sell them for tax purposes.

- The winners are already in your portfolio.
  Do not sell your winners as they may turn into bigger winners unless you have a good reason. Do not sell them if they still pass your recent stock analysis. During any market plunge, you may want to sell them but you should buy them back when the market recovers.

When you mismatch the strategy with market conditions, you will lose the opportunity for profit or even lose money. If the market is up or down steadily, a side way strategy will not work. Matching the strategy to the current market conditions is not an easy job and sometimes it takes some luck. However, when it matches, it would be firework. If you match more times than you miss, you should make good money.

8   Refined Dogs of Dow

What is it?

Dogs of Dow (http://en.wikipedia.org/wiki/The_Dogs_of_the_Dow) is quite popular and even some mutual fund managers are using it exclusively. In a nutshell, you buy the ten Dow stocks that pay the highest dividend rates at year end and repeat the process every year. Ignore the stocks whose dividends are returns of capital. Click the above hyperlink for more info on this strategy.

Past Performance

As of 2012, it just beats Dow and S&P500 by a small margin in last decade except the last two years

The better performance of this strategy over the last two years could be due to the recent mild bubble on dividend growth stocks and most of those dogs belong to this group. Hence, be alert to when the dividend bubble bursts.

From Wikipedia,

"In fact, the Dogs of the Dow and Small Dogs of the Dow struggled to keep up with the Dow during latter stages of the dot-com boom (1998 and 1999) as well as during the financial crisis (2007-2009)."

Improve the performance as suggested in this book
1. Avoid stocks with high expected P/Es such as most dot-com stocks in 2000.

2. Avoid sectors as described in Chapter 6 such as banks in 2007.

3. Practice market timing.

Improve the performance by customizing

When a strategy becomes popular, it will not perform due to the herd mentality (http://tonyp4idea.blogspot.com/2011/12/fool-of-all-fools.html).

Customize the strategy so that I do not pick the identical stocks as others who use the identical strategy.

Instead of buying the ten dogs, buy the first five dogs sorted by the forward (same as expected) positive P/E in ascending order and ignoring stocks with negative earnings.

This variation has an average annualized return of 15% (12% appreciation + estimated 3% dividend) from Nov. 1, 2000 to Nov. 1, 2010 from my testing. It is better than the original strategy already.

Another variation is: Buy the top five candidates on Nov. 1 and sell them on May 1 next year to benefit from the statistically favorable period.

Further Refining Dogs of Dow

The following are the variations to the original Dogs of Dow. Try one or more combinations.

1. Include the stocks in S&P 500 and NASDAQ, so there are more stocks to choose from.

2. Adjust the time between Dec. 1 and Dec. 15 (a little earlier is fine) instead of the start of the year to avoid the herd who follows the same strategy and performs the same task at the beginning of the year.

3. For retirement accounts or offsetting the short-term losers, try to buy on Nov.1 and sell on May 1 to take advantage of this normally favorable period.

4. Sort the selected top 10 with positive earnings by P/E in ascending order and buy the top 5. A value play. I prefer to skip P/E less than 4 as there may be something wrong with the company.

5. Avoid stocks in the following sectors: lenders, drug companies, miners, insurers and emerging countries as described in Chapter 6.

6. Skip the companies that have serious lawsuits against them. Minor lawsuits are fine.

7. Avoid stocks that are being shorted in the range of 10% to 20%. The short % is defined by: No. of shares being shorted/Total floating shares. Stocks with short percent over 30% could trigger a short squeeze that could have great appreciation potential.

8. Use stop loss when the market is at the peak phase of the market cycle. For a better understanding of this, read one of my several books described in Appendix 5 (Debunk the Myths in Investing, Debunk the Myths in Investing for Couch Potatoes and Market Timing: 3P.

9. Do not buy on the first year after the market plunge.

It is a lazy man's stock picking and market timing. I bet it performs better than the original strategy.

Afterthoughts

*

When you test the above strategy, try different parameters. If possible, use the most recent data (such as the last five years) to check out whether your strategy still works. If you are less risk tolerant, select the strategy such as low P/E that may produce poorer performance but has less maximum drawback (i.e. the highest % of loss from the highest of the year).

The following are some of the variance and can be combined into this strategy.

-Holding periods. Try 6 months, 11 months and 12 months.
- Buy contra ETFs during the unfavorable stock period such as May 1 to Nov. 1.

- Automatic as much the testing as possible, so you can add other parameters such as different holding periods.

- Avoid data fitting to obtain better results.
- Test for each stage of the market cycle.

*

Annualize the return if it is not 12 months for easier to compare. Do not get too excited on great returns. When you implement your strategy with real money, expect to beat the market by a small percentage only.

Review your test procedures when the return is excessive such as 60%. However, when you find one strategy yielding 60% and another one yielding 20% with same testing conditions, stick with the winner for real money.

Start with paper trading and then with a small portfolio.

There is no Holy Grail in investing. The market changes and it is not rational all the time otherwise there would be no poor folks.
Investing with a good strategy is better than investing without one.

*

Tom said:
Like every trading strategy, when everyone starts practicing it, the "advantage" goes away. We saw that plain and clear in 2008-09. Since nearly all financial advisors practice this discipline, it is no surprise to me that all correlations are slowly drifting to "1", and will probably stay that way until MPT losses steam.

[Tony: That's why I modified the original Dogs of Dow. I believe mine performs better and at less risk. As in any strategy, there is no guarantee.]

9   Super safe strategies

These strategies are for orphans and widows. The common theme is that you want to spend very little time in investing. There are better things to do than investing. You may not have the knowledge in investing or the desire to learn about investing. However, most likely the safe strategies do not beat inflation except the last strategy described in this article.

Strategy #1: CD and long-term treasury bills

They are virtually risk-free. Even if it takes almost no-effort for the strategy except in renewing the expired CDs, I still recommend some actions:

- Do not invest in a CD with a bank that you have already exceeded the government's limit on insurance. As of 2019, the standard deposit insurance coverage limit is **$250,000** per depositor, per FDIC-insured bank and per ownership category.

- Today's CDs do not beat inflation. It is our capitalist system that punishes us for not taking any risk and effort in investing.

- Some mortgage-backed bonds or similar offerings could lose all the potential value as many found out the hard way from Lehman Brother's bonds disguised as safe CDs.
- Do not buy callable CDs. They will be called to the bank's advantages.

- Buy long-term treasury bills when the interest rates is high (say 5% or higher). Buy short-term treasury bills when the interest rates is low (say less than 2%). Although you can receive your entire principle plus interest when they mature, the value of the bond fluctuates in opposite directions to the current rate. When the current interest rates is better than the one in your treasury bill, your bill will depreciate.

- Most folks buy the treasury bills via mutual funds and/or ETFs.

Strategy #2: Annuity

When you retire, it seems to be a good vehicle to buy an annuity to provide income for life. However, you have to understand the annuities' terms are defined by the sellers with their own agenda. If you believe they're in business to make you a comfortable retirement at their own expenses, think again. Very few if any are low-expense operations. Ask how much the salesman would make to sell you the annuity, and most likely you would run to the door for quick exit.

I invested in an annuity when I was working to postpone my taxes for the gains. It could be a mistake for me even I made over 4 times during several decades. My taxes after 70 ½ (the age for mandatory withdrawal of retirement accounts) will be higher than my working years. I did well in rotating sectors (offered in my annuity) partly due to luck. The total expenses (the trading fees and the management fees) are not cheap compared to most ETFs.

It is good when you have better things to do in your life than worrying about the market. It would save some taxes if your tax bracket is lowered after retirement (as most folks do). If we have a market plunge, then these two strategies would be a winner.

Strategy #3: Rotation of an ETF and cash

Rotate between SPY (or any ETF that simulates the market) and cash (or a short-term treasury bond ETF). When the market is risky, rotate your investment into cash and vice versa for SPY. This book describes market timing; it is quite simple.

For beginners, it appears more complicated than it is. You only spend several minutes every month. You will beat most mutual fund managers as most of them are not allowed to play market timing. To start, allocate a small percentage of your investing to this strategy or test the strategy on paper. There is some risk due to false signals. However, "nothing risked, nothing gained" is quite true especially for the long term.

10   Tom's conservative strategy

The following is a summary of Tom's conservative strategy as described in his profile on Seeking Alpha web site. Use it as an example and modify it to fit your investing philosophy. You need to ignore your friends telling you how much money he is making when the market is up. You also need not tell them how much money you're not losing, otherwise you will not have any friends.

Click here (for Kindle readers) for Tom's strategy. (http://tonyp4idea.blogspot.com/2012/05/tom-armisteads-investment-strategy.html)

Ignore the date posted as this is one of the very few strategies that are evergreen. As of 12/2015, it does not perform well during 2009 (or 2010) to 2015 due to the long, unexpected rising market. However, it beats the above two strategies by good margins in the long run.

A winning strategy for couch potatoes

My friend John has a very similar strategy similar to Tom's. My friend is making money with the least risk. He only buys stocks after the market crashes and sell stocks when the market rises. Ignore all market pundits. This is recommended to anyone who does not have time to monitor his/her investment.

He bought stocks in 2008-2010 and sold them after 2010. It was very profitable for him in 2000-2008 using this simple strategy. However, he missed the gains from 2010 to 2018. It is unusual that we have such a long bull market. I beg he is still beating most mutual fund managers with this simple strategy that does not require much work.

Enhance a good strategy

Following the favorable stages to trade in the market cycle described in this book:
- Buy SPY in the Early Recovery phase (about 1 ½ year after the crash or use the entry point described in Market Timing in this book.
- Sell SPY in one or two years after the buy.

Here are some options if you have time to watch the market.

- Buy stocks (or an ETF that simulates the market) in Nov. 1 and sell them in May 1. I prefer to buy stocks on Oct. 15 and sell them on April 15 to avoid the herd.
- Buy stocks on Dec. 1 and sell them on Feb. 1 to take advantage of the best (statistically) period of the year.
- Buy stocks in the year before the election and sell them after a year.
- Add long-term bonds when the interest rates is high (say more than 5%). Switch to short-term bonds or cash when the interest rates is low (say less than 2%).
- If you have time, time the market by following my simple technique to exit and reenter the market.

Spend the rest of the time on your comfortable couch (i.e. enjoying life) or sip some fancy tropical drink served by some beautiful tropical lady on some nice tropical island. Not a bad strategy! Of course, the market is not always rational and there is always risk involved.

An alternative to Tom's strategy

Have a list of value stocks to buy and update the list periodically (say every 3 months).

When the market loses 5%, buy them at 2% less than the market prices or alternatively 5% less than the prices on your list.

Decide when to sell such as making 12% profit or losing 12%. If the market is not risky, you may want to keep them longer. It should work in a sideways market but not during market plunges.

John's Strategy

John maintains about 75% cash and only buys blue chip stocks at 52-week low. He ignores friends telling him about making good money when the market is up.

Here are my changes for better returns at the expense of taking more risk. I would maintain 50% cash and 0% in Early Recovery, a phase in the market cycle defined by me. I would also include all stocks with market cap over 1 billion and stocks close to 5% of their bottoms. In addition, I would evaluate the stocks before I buy as some stocks may go to zero.

Jill's Strategy

Jill does not have time for investing. She subscribes to an investing service. She prepares a list of stocks to buy. For illustration purposes only, the stocks should have Safety of 1 or 2 in Value Line or VST grade higher than 1.25 in Vector Vest. When the price reaches the price she is willing to pay, she does a second research with her subscription service and check the fundamental rating at Fidelity.com. If they are good, she buys it and usually keeps it until the market is risky.

#Filler: Miss Mia

In my first job just after the Vietnam War, every one tried to date my beautiful office mate Mia except me. If we married, then her name would be Mia Pow. She would be very popular, or very unpopular without showing her beautiful face. In any case, when she becomes a mother, she will be Mamma Mia.

BTW. I was the "comfort man" due to the gender gap during the Vietnam War.

11   Year-end strategies

I have two: 1. Buy the current year winners (YEW) and 2. Buy the current year losers (YEL).

The first strategy is riding the institutional investors' window dressing to include the winners in their funds to make them look better.

The second strategy takes advantage of selling losers for tax purposes. We need to find value stocks, not stocks that are heading to bankruptcy.

The following describes how to create your own testing if you have a historical database. It would be a frame of testing other strategies.

- Define the starting date. For the first strategy, I would use 10/1 and 11/1 for two sets of test. For the second strategy, I would use 12/1 and 12/15. Check which starting date is better for the specific strategy.
- Define the durations, the number of months before you sell the bought stocks. I use 2 months, 4 months, 6 months and 12 months for the durations.
- Define the numbers of tests. I start from 2000, one or two years older if your historical database allows. However, do not use dates older than 1995 as the market was quite different then.
- Compare your results to SPY (or the S&P 500 index).
- Ignore dividends for simplicity.
- Use annualized rates for better comparison.
- If the date has no data such as holidays and weekends, use the date after it for consistency.
- Take out stocks that would not be the stocks you usually buy, penny stocks (that likely boost the performance due to survivorship bias), small foreign companies and/or stocks giving huge dividends or giving return of capital.
- Use different metric to sort, such as Expected Earning Yield (E/P) or a composite grade. Use the top 10 (or 5) stocks.

- Include maximum drawback (the maximum loss) from many selected durations. My maximum loss is -52% from 12/1/2007 to one year later in my Year-End Loss strategy, but followed by 256% gain in the next year.
- Negative percent numbers could give wrong calculations comparing to the index. Check them out manually if your formula has not taken care of the negative numbers.
- Here are my best results for the two strategies. Again, my results will not be the same as yours due to different selections. Past performances may have nothing to do with future performances.

The year-end loser strategy in 2015 does not work that well as I screened many stocks that are scored very low. I found out many screened stocks are foreign countries. Many emerging countries have problems and I do not trust most of their financial info. Besides that, many are energy companies that I already have too many.

Many have Expected Earning Yields over 35%. However, most have very high debts such as Debt/Equity is over 1 (i.e. 100%). If I bought them, I would unload them in 3 months fearing a market crash in 2016. Historically, it is profitable, but I may skip most YEL stocks this year as most are deserved losers. The lesson is: Adjust to the current market conditions.

Strategy	Starting Date	Duration	Avg. Annual. %	Max. Drawn Down
YE Winners	10/1	4 months	40%	-36%
YE Losers	12/1	6 months	42%	-28%

My experience

Making good money needs to find a strategy that matches to the current market. Here are my recent strategies I actually tried with money in 2018.

* Window dressing for institutional investors from Nov. 1 to Dec. 1 (some use dates earlier than Nov. 1). Buy current winners and sell current losers of stocks with large market cap.

The market was risky so I did not buy winners but shorted some losers.

* Buy year-end losers from Nov. 1 to Dec. 31 (some use dates earlier than Nov.1). The companies have to be profitable (>15%), big losers (most having over 50% yearly loss) and small companies (preferred).

Incorporate the strategy with today's volatile market (i.e. buy when they plunge and sell when they rise). Determine what is "plunge" and "rise". For me, it is short-term and the percent is 5% from recent high or low.

There is a selling part of these strategies I have not included here. Most of my strategies are based on exhaustive tests from historical data with a lot of work.

Every market is different. We need to make a lot of adjustments. From my experiences, the best research may not make you money all the time. In the long run, the more educated your work, the better chance of making money.

Year-End 2018

This is one of my best monthly returns. The average purchase date is 12/27/2018 and the current prices were based on 1/28/2019. The return is 53% and 648% annualized. Most likely the performance will not be repeated. However, it serves as a procedure for coming years.

I change the quantity Q to 1. Several stocks have been purchased more than once. Sold 3 stocks already with Status = 'Sold'.

Account	Screen	Year-end loser	Start	12/21/19	End	1/8/2019 Today	1/28/19				
Stock	Q	Buy	Sell	Buy $	Sell $	Buy Date	Sell Date	# Days	Profit $	Profit %	Ann %	Status
401KC											
CHK	1	2.13	2.99	2	3	01/03/19	01/18/19	15	1	40%	982% Sold
MNK	1	16.41	21.45	16	21	01/03/19	01/25/19	22	5	31%	510% Sold
MNK	1	16.43	21.45	16	21	01/03/19	01/25/19	22	5	31%	507% Sold
NNBR	1	5.68	8.58	6	9	12/26/18	01/28/19	33	3	51%	565%
NNBR	1	5.72	8.58	6	9	12/26/18	01/28/19	33	3	66%	727%
ESTE	1	4.35	6.45	4	6	12/26/18	01/18/19	23	2	48%	766% Sold
JT											
LCI	1	4.61	8.29	5	8	12/21/18	01/28/19	38	4	80%	767%
MDR	1	8.01	9.13	8	9	01/08/19	01/28/19	20	1	14%	255%
YRCW	1	3.29	5.78	3	6	12/21/18	01/28/19	38	2	76%	727%
YRCW	1	3.26	5.78	3	6	12/21/18	01/28/19	38	3	77%	742%
401K											
ASRT	1	3.56	4.18	4	4	12/26/18	01/28/19	33	1	17%	193%
UTCC	1	7.13	11.00	7	11	12/26/18	01/28/19	33	4	54%	600%
YRCW	1	2.92	5.78	3	6	12/26/18	01/28/19	33	3	98%	1083%
Tot/avg				84	119	12/27/18		29	36	53%	648%

I sold my YRCW (not shown above) on the earnings date that can be found in Finviz.com. It is a mistake. If the earnings are positive, it will be sold for my asking price plus a little more but less than the surge. If it is negative, it will not be sold. Recommend to cancel the sell order before the earnings date.

As of 09/07/2019, LCI is up by 185% and YRCW is down by 27% (I sold one position in my retirement account for about 100% gain).

How long should we hold these screened stocks?

Except those in taxable account, I sold all of them in the first two months. The following is the annualized returns for holding 1 month, 2 months, 3 months and 5 months (as of 6/22/2019). From my previous testing, I should hold the stocks for 6 months. However, I have made my objective already and I want to take advantage of this volatile market.

I could not find UTCC in my historical database. I sold it with an annualized return of 572%. It could be acquired or merged. For simplicity, I used 12/27/2018 as the purchase dates for all stocks. I consider one position for each stock and hence 3 purchases of YRCW is considered at one purchase. Again, I do not include dividends, the bid spread and commissions.

	1 Month	2 Months	3 Months	5 Months
Ann. Return	497%	366%	178%	17%
SPY	72%	74%	52%	31%

From the above, I did well in selling most of them. If I held all of them for 5 months, they would not beat the SPY, the market to many.

Fillers

- First bought or sold by insiders and their relatives, then followed by programmed computers, institutional investors, technicians and retail investors.
- Missed to short PG&E and VALE when the news broke. There is more in life than playing the market
- The shutdown costs more than enough to build Trump's Great Wall of America. How stupid the politicians can be? How stupid are the voters? Do not vote for the politicians who use shutdown as a tool!!!

12   Top-down investing

The nutshell is described here. Only buy stocks when the market is favorable. Find the best industry (a subsector) and then find the best stock(s) within the selected industry. In doing so, our chances of successful investing are substantially increased.

It is so simple and it has been proven by many including myself. I just wonder why it has not been extensively practiced. I offer a simple trading plan as follows:

1. Do not invest when the market is plunging. I have a simple way to detect market plunges without any expensive subscriptions or tools.

2. Select the best industry (most are represented by an ETF or ETFs specific for the industry or sector). For example, Technology is a sector. Computer and Software are industries (subsector under Technology). From time to time I use sectors for simplicity and most free sites do not sub divide the sectors into industries. Check out the best-performing industry or sector from last month in many sites including SeekingAlpha and CNNfn.

    If you're a value investor, you may not want to choose the timeliest sector but the most under-valued sector. Value investors should hold the sectors/stocks longer (such as 6 months or even longer) for the market to recognize their values.

    In addition, you need to detect the sector/stock rotation by the institutional investors who control over 75% of all trades (i.e. smart money). They will rotate sector/stock when they find better profit potential in another sector/stock. Use stops to prevent further losses.

    If you do not have time to research on stocks, trade ETFs for sectors and skip the next step.

3. The final step is to select the best stock(s) within the sector via fundamental analysis (including intangible analysis), insider trading analysis, institution trading analysis and technical analysis.

   Do not let these terms scare you. We will start with the simplest approach without any subscription and a lot of effort.

4. The next step is when to reevaluate and sell the stocks when conditions change or they meet your objectives. If the market is plunging, sell all stocks.

Stick with and repeat the entire process.

The easiest retirement planning system

Have a budget and live within your means. Buy good stuff that lasts for a long time. After saving enough cash for emergency and planned expenses such as vacation, new car, college, etc., invest your extra money in a retirement account (Roth IRA if allowable) with 80% in a market ETF and 20% in a short-term bond ETF.

Run the chart described in the market cycle chapters once a month. If the chart tells you to exit the market, move all to cash. Reenter the market when the chart tells you to do so. It beats most if not all of your financial plans from the best experts money can buy.

Afterthoughts

My late friend had a 'buy and hold strategy' that worked pretty well. Most of his stocks were big companies. He died with a house worth more than a million and many millions in stocks. His only mistake was not to transfer more of his stocks to his heirs before his death. He died on the year when the estate exemption returned back to a million. Uncle Sam was the biggest winner and won big without any effort.

13   A turnaround strategy for value stocks

Many value stocks tend to stay in this phase for a long time. When the turnaround starts, it could be very profitable.

Market Timing

Do not buy any stock when the market is risky as described elsewhere in the book. Actually you should sell most of the stocks when the market is risky.

Buy Metrics

Metric	Value	Conservative	Aggressive
General			
Market Cap	>300 M	>1,000 M	>100 M
Price	> 2	>10	>1
Avg. Volume	>20,000	>50,000	>10,000
USA	Only	Only	Foreign but listed in USA
Fundamental			
Forward P/E	<15	<10	<25
Earning Gr Q-Q	>5%	>8%	>3%
ROE	>10	>15	>5
P / FCF	<10	<8	<15
Debt / Equity	<.5	<.25	<1
Technical			
SMA-50%	>10	>15	>5
Misc.			
Blue Chip Growth	A or B	A	A or B
Fidelity	>6	>8	>5
IBD	>60	>90	>50
Vector Vest	>=1	>=0.8	>=12
Value Line Proj. 3-5% return	>5%	>10%	>5%
Zacks	>=4	5	>=4
ASSS	>=2	>=5	>=2

The assignment values for the metrics are not fixed; feel free to change it according to your own risk level. I do have suggestions for conservative investors and aggressive investors.

Some of the metrics are not readily available in Finviz.com and the following describes how to modify them.

Explanation

- Market Cap. The free version of Finviz.com does not allow you to specify the range. Use 'Any' and then select the stocks according to the specified values. Average Volume has the similar restriction.
- The conservative values for Market Cap, Price and Average Volume try to select larger companies. The aggressive values try to select smaller companies, which historically are more risky but perform better.
- I prefer 'USA' for Country. Stay away from small companies from developing countries unless you can trust their financial statements.
- Forward P/E measures the value of the stock. Ensure "E" (Earnings) is positive. I prefer it over P/E (from the last twelve months).
- Earnings Growth Quarter to last Quarter is preferred to be positive unless it is during a recession.
- ROE measures how well the company has been managed.
- P/FCF. "Price / Free Cash Flow" cannot be manipulated easily. Together with low "Debt / Equity", it measures whether the company would bankrupt.
- SMA-50%. Some stocks tend to stay in a value stage for a long while (termed value trap). We like to select stocks just starting being noticed and on its way up.
- Misc. Many sites have evaluated the stocks for us. Some only let their customers to access such information, some are available for free trials or are available from the library.
- ASSS is my scoring system.

With the above, I have 35 stocks on 10/28/16. If you need 10 stocks for further evaluation, try to sort Forward P/E in descending order and select the top 10. If you cannot find any or substantially less than normal, it implies the market is risky, so take a break. If the performances of the last few stocks you selected are poor, take a break too as the market conditions do not favor the value metrics we specified.

Qualitative analysis

Double click on the stock and read as many articles described on the stock as possible. If it meets all the criteria, buy the stock. Recommend to use market orders for large companies in a non-volatile market (when the average daily fluctuation is less than 0.5%). If the selected stock is the one you just sold, make you only buy it after 31 days to avoid Wash Sale penalty.

Keeping informed

Check the company updates of the stock you owned every month. One easy way is to enter the stocks in a portfolio in SeekingAlpha.com.

Sell the stock

Re-evaluate the stocks every 6 months.

If it does not meet the criteria or the market is risky, sell it. If it is only a few days away from the long-term capital gain, sell the losers right away or hold on the winner for a few more days.

Re-balance the portfolio after a stock has been sold. Ensure it is diversified enough into large/small cap and sectors.

Top-down Investing

It is similar to the above. Find the sectors that perform the best last month. Under Finviz.com, select the best sector under 'sector' one at a time. Several sites such as Fidelity compare the stock to the averages of stocks in the same sector.

Section VII: Trading stocks

We sell stocks when the reasons to buy no longer apply by a good margin. In most cases, the sell decision should be based more than one quarter.

I sold ALU when it gained 40% in a few weeks. It gained more than 300% later when it was acquired. For rising stocks, we should adjust the stop orders. Do it mentally (i.e. not placing stop orders) to avoid flash crashes and/or using trailing stops.

1   Order prices

Market orders
It is simply trading the stock at the prevailing market price. Place market orders only when it is necessary as stocks price can easily be manipulated especially on stocks with low trading volumes. To avoid manipulations, do not place market orders after hours.

However, in a rising market, many fast rising stocks can only be bought via market orders. Many winners never take a breather on their way up. In this case, you can only buy the stock via market orders.

Consider bid and ask. A 'bid' is the price a potential buyer would like to buy while the 'ask' is a potential seller would like to sell. Your market price is usually the worst price in either case, but it is a guarantee that you would trade the stock. A large spread would mean that it would take a longer time to use a limit order and/or the trade volume of the stock is small.

In my momentum portfolio on 11/2013, I placed a sell price for GERN far higher than the market price. Surprisingly I sold it for this price making an annualized return of 1,176% for holding it for 21 days. When there are few or no other sellers for the stock, the market price would be the price you set. If I cannot sell it in the next 9 days (30 days is my holding period for momentum stocks), I would set it lower. Update: One year later, GERN lost 29%.

Sensible discounts
I prefer to buy the stock at the price closest to the last trade price (to most it is the market price) via a limit order. I seldom lose buying

these orders. Sometimes I use the day's lowest price to buy (or the highest to sell) plus a penny (or minus a penny for sell prices to sell).

My other purchase strategy is using 0.15% or 0.25% less than the current prices for stocks I really want. For some promising stocks, I buy them at almost the market price and then place another order on the same stock at 0.5% less than the last traded price (and sometimes 2% depending on the current market trend).

We all want to buy less and sell at higher prices. However, if the trade price is too far away from the current market price (such as 5% from the market price), these trades may never be executed. I have had a long list of buy orders that were not executed and turned out to be big gainers. Learn from my bad experiences.

Use a good discount (such as 10% from the market price) if you believe the market, the sector or the stock will dip by 10%. After you bought the stock, you place a sell order 10% more than the price you paid for it hoping the stock will return to the original price and you pocket 10%. Wishful thinking! However, it has happened to me several times primarily due to temporary market dips.

It works when there is a correction and/or the stock is very volatile. It is usually within the 5% range to take advantage of these situations, not the 10% as described. For a 10% plunge, it usually is due to some serious problem of the company surfacing. One common reason is not meeting its earnings expectation and in this case it usually continues its downward trend.

Larger discounts on a falling market
During a falling market (or a mild correction), 3% less than the current prices for buy orders may be fine for some stocks (use 5% for volatile stocks). To illustrate, I placed about 10 of these orders over the last two months during a market dip. Most of the orders were filled. When the market is plunging, do not buy any stock.

Caterpillar and Cisco were some of my buys at these discounts. They were in my watch list to buy. Initially these shares often fall even lower as the trend was downward. As of 12/18/12, CAT earned me from 3% and 14% (bought in 6/12 and 7/12) and CSCO bought in 7/14/12 returned about 34%. My original objective: Buy deeply-valued stocks, wait and sell them when the economy returns.

When you predict the market will dip by 5%, set your buy orders accordingly. Again, predictions are just educated guesses. From my experience, they work most of the time but not all of the time.

On the day of the earnings announcement, the fluctuation of the stock is usually high. Check any change in the earnings estimate before the announcement and act accordingly. Zacks is supposed to be a useful tool to predict earnings estimates. Do not leave orders during the earnings announcement dates, which can be found in Finviz. When the earning turns out to be good, the stock price surges and your order will not be executed. When the earnings are bad, the stock price will plunge usually and you most likely over-payed.

Option expiration dates usually cause more volatility. Retail investors do not have to be concerned except you may use wider stops. In theory, dividend days have little effect on the stock price as it will be lowered by the dividend amount.

High volume of a stock could mean opportunity

High volume usually increases the stock price volatility. If the volatility of a stock increases substantially (such as doubling its average daily volume), there could be important news on the company, recommendation changes from a major analyst or trading by the institutional investors. It usually takes the institutional investors a week to trade a stock with their sizable positions.

Many times it is started by the insiders who know about the breaking news of a stock before it is publicized. Some investment services / sites specialize in identifying the increasing volumes on these stocks.

Because day traders do not want to leave any open positions overnight, higher volatility occurs at the end of the day. It is the same on the day (usually on Friday) when the options are expiring.

Monitor your trade prices
You cannot tell whether you are paying a fair price without keeping a record. To illustrate, you're paying 1% less than the market prices in buying stocks. You may have missed buying some winners. If the 1% you saved is smaller than the appreciation of the stocks you

would have bought at market prices, then you should adjust the buy prices to 0.5% less than the market price and monitor again.

Market trend makes a difference too. When the market is trending up, buying any stock would most likely be profitable and usually the purchase orders with higher discounts will not be executed.

Follow the same logic on sell orders. Need to have at least 25 stock purchases (and potential purchases) to make the conclusion meaningful. If you do not trade a lot, you will not have enough data to verify. As described, I prefer not to place an order during the earnings announcement dates which can be found in Finviz.com. If you cannot buy the stock, consider to use market order the next day. With most brokers offer no commission trades, the "All or none" option is not valid.

Good prospects

When you find gems especially those stocks that are followed by analysts, buy them at market prices and consider doubling the bet if you are really sure you have a winner. From my super stock screens, I spotted NHTC. I placed several bets and one market order. All of them were NOT executed except with the market order. At the end of the day NHTC is up 18% and my executed order is up 14%. I did not have the best buy but made a good profit. NHTC was on its way to a huge appreciation and I sold it too early. I have earned not to sell a winner and protect the profit with a stop.

Lower the buy for risky stocks (if the beta from Finviz is greater than 1 for example) even if they have good fundamentals.

Quality over quantity

If your time is limited, spend all the time on researching one stock one at a time. However, you need to own at least 3 stocks (more stocks for a large portfolio) for your diversification purposes.

Double your normal purchase position on stocks that look great after the research. For risky stocks that look good, you may want to halve your normal purchase position to cut down on the risk. If you are less risk tolerant, do not buy risky stocks at all. My results are not conclusive on risky stocks but I do get a good sleep.

2   Stop loss & flash crash

You can limit your stock loss with stops. There are some incidents where you do not always want to use a stop loss.

- <u>Flash crash</u> (May 6, 2010 and August 2015).
It would turn your stops into market orders that could be substantially lower than your stop prices. Some brokers offer stop limits, but they do not guarantee the orders will be executed.

  The better way is a "mental stop" (my term). You do not place a stop order but place a market order to sell when your stock falls below a pre-defined price. During flash crashes, you do not want to place the market orders to sell but place orders to buy from your watch list.

  I bought some stocks at more than 10% discount during the flash crash (actually I could buy them even at better discounts) and within a week most had returned to the prices as before the flash crash.

  Placing buy orders with huge discounts to the market prices works better for volatile stocks. You should cancel the unexecuted trades before the weekends / holidays and reenter them afterwards to avoid unexpected events that may affect the stock prices.

  Avoid trading drug and bio tech companies with huge differences to the market prices. High tech is a good sector for this purpose and fluctuating 10% in this sector is more of a norm than an exception. Buying an ETF at 5% discount is a better bet than buying specific stocks from my experience.

- My experience with 911.
I sold many stocks due to stop orders during 911. The market came back in the next three days and I missed the recovery from the stocks that were sold and did not buy back them in time.

- If your stocks are rising, you need to adjust the stop loss prices accordingly. To illustrate- in maintaining a 10% stop loss, your stop is at 90 when the current price is 100. When the stock price rises to 200, it should be adjusted to $180 (10% less than the current price). It is also called a trailing stop. Need to review these rising stocks, and change the stop price periodically (one week to one month depending on how volatile is the stock)).

Most brokers allow you to enter most trades "Good till Cancelled". Even for that there is an expiration date such as 6 months for Fidelity. Fidelity's trades for Short Sell expire by the end of the trade session. Check your broker's current policy.

- Risky markets.
  When the market is risky, you may want to use a stop loss. To prevent another flash crash, you may want to use a 'mental' market order. It is not perfect, as it requires constant watching of the market.

  There are many investing services and sites that give you the 'right' prices for a stop loss. Basically it depends on how volatile are the specific stocks. The chartists will tell you under normal conditions stocks are trading between the resistance line and the support line. Use the stop loss just below the resistance line to avoid the stop order from being executed due to the volatility of the stock.

  For simplicity as I have too many stocks in my portfolio, I use a percent. In the old days, it was recommended 8% or so below the prices you paid. In today's volatile market, I recommend 12%.

- Risky stocks.
  A stop loss is the only way that you can limit your loss for big drop (such as 25%). Affimax lost 85% of its stock value in one day with the news that three of its patients died.

- Low-volume stocks.
  The market order could drive the prices right down as there are few buyers in low-volume stocks. If there is only one buyer, he will buy with the best price for him (or the worst price to the seller).

Unless I have good reasons, I would skip the low-volume stocks. I define low-volume: If my buy amount is higher than 1% of the average daily amount (= average daily volume * stock price).

- Beta.
  Stocks may be more volatile than the market. Beta is used to measure its volatility. The market can be measured by the S&P500 index. If the beta of a stock is 1, its volatility is the same as the market. If it is 1.2, it is 20% more volatile.

  Set a lower stop loss for volatile stocks to prevent stocks from selling due to regular fluctuations.

Afterthoughts

Let me show you my bitter experience. The following are 5 stocks I wanted to buy and the average return was quite good.

Stocks	Return
URI	63%
GMCR	572%
MTW	186%
PII	-74%
TSCO	-127%
Avg.	124%

I placed buy orders at 5% less than the market prices as most 'bargain' investors do. I bought both of the two losers but no winners. The winners never took a breather on its way up, but the losers went down. I did buy GMCR via a market order in my momentum strategy in a separate account.

3   Brokers

Protect the security of your financial transactions. Do not hit any web link that you do not know including those 'good' deals – your greed could cause you to lose millions! I use my Chrome for these transactions and I do not access my e-mails via this Chrome. A two-step log in (if available) should be useful. The broker sends you a temporary log-in password to your mobile phone. Install anti-virus software such as Norton and Malwarebytes. Do not use the mobile phone for trading stocks and stay away from 'free Wi-Fi' networks. Besides your broker account, tax info, bank accounts and credit card are the next important things that you need to protect.

Today most brokers are discount brokers. Choose one to start with and two should be the maximum.

The following is for illustration purposes only as I should not recommend any broker. Fidelity offers a lot of research free and commission-free trades (similar to Charles Schwab), extensive mutual funds and bank/credit card services. Interactive Broker has a low margin rate (vs. Fidelity's 9% or so today) and low commissions on some transactions. Many others have their own advantages. If you only need one broker, select the one based on your requirements.

Today many brokers offer many trading options that were not available 15 years ago such as trading a stock with specific condition(s) and canceling an order based on certain condition(s). For example, you can have a stop order and a limited sell order on the same stock.

Full-service brokers offer some services most discount brokers do not offer. One offers buying IPO stocks and selling them automatically at the end of the day. This strategy had been doing well except in 2015. Do not believe you can pay someone to manage your portfolio and you're all set. There have been cases of portfolio churning to generate income for the broker.

There are many magazine articles comparing brokers. I do not really care whether the order is executed in 1 or 5 micro seconds. However, I do find some orders have been traded better by one broker over another. What do you mean 'by traded better' you may ask? The followings are examples. I cannot prove whether they are true or not but to me, it seems to be true.

- I have identical buy orders placed with two brokers. Consistently one broker gets them executed more often than the other broker.
- One broker often gives me better prices than the other. For example, my sell price was $10, and many times I got more than $10 such as $10.02.
- One broker has more reversed orders than the other. For example, I was informed my order was executed but they told me it had been reversed on the second day.
- One consistently charged extra fees. I understand it is tough to make the paper-thin commissions today.
- ADR fees. Some are quite hefty. I avoid many foreign stocks. Some charge more for the gains especially France. At one time, most ADR stocks did well, but not anymore as the US stocks have been doing well (as of 2/2017). The ADR fees are charged by your broker or bank. The following is from a Kiplinger's article.

"ADRs, which represent shares of ownership in a foreign company, trade in the U.S. in dollars. Some ADRs come with a contractual provision that allows the broker, in this case TD Ameritrade, to levy "depositary services fees."

The charges, commonly 2 cents per share, are intended to cover the cost of coordinating overseas investments. For ADRs that include this provision, the broker can levy the charge at any time, but no more than once a year. "

Margin
Margin should not be used extensively. It is expensive and most brokers try every trick to squeeze profits from all transactions to subsidize their low-commission incomes. Usually you can borrow up to 40% of your current position and the margin rates vary among brokers. Check out your broker's margin rate. In general, margin is not allowed in your retirement accounts. You may need to file an application for margin. Your brokers ensure you meet specific requirements to lower their risk such as your income.

Many lost a lot during the last two market plunges. However, many including myself made a killing in 2003 and 2009 using margin. I use it for the following reasons. For convenience in placing buy orders that exceed my cash position in my taxable accounts.

Tips and tricks

- Many brokers' promotions offers you cash and/or free trades (not longer needed as many brokers offer commission-free trades) if you deposit a specific amount in your account. Without commission cost, you do not need to round up to a lot size (100 shares in most cases) nor specify "All or None". Check the details of the offers. Some give you free trades only up to 60 days while others offer up to two years.
- Some brokers restrict withdrawal in a specific time frame such as one year or during the period of the free commission. After that, you can move it to another broker that gives you similar deals. In most cases, the offer is per social security number or per person. A bad execution of a trade is not worth the free commission and/or any goodies.
- If you need margin a lot such as shorting stocks, check out the margin rates from different brokers.
- Most brokers offer basic trading lessons and market reviews. Most are well-written.
- Most brokers offer stock evaluation. Some are really good with proven records. Take advantage of it.
- Many brokers offer two-phase logon for better security. Many send you a security code to your mobile phone or your email account. Then you enter the code.
- Ignore filling out the forms for group lawsuits unless your stock holding is large. I received $20 for spending at least 2 hours to find my statement.
- Today it is not relevant to most brokers as they are already commission-free. So is the "All but none" option during entering a trade.
- Some brokers may require you to confirm if you want to trade using margin, options, penny stocks, risky stocks and after-hour trading.

4   Fidelity

On 10/2019, Fidelity announced there was no commission for most trades.

I have been satisfied with the trades so far. It is more important to me than commissions. One broker offered free trades for keeping a balance. However, there are many times the orders that should be executed have not been executed. More than 2 times, the completed orders have been reversed. I have not had this with Fidelity so far and actually some orders have been executed with better prices. Fidelity passes the best price to you while some brokers keep the difference for themselves.

As with most major brokers, Turbo Tax can load all my stock transactions for the year in filing my tax returns. It saves me a lot of time. Fidelity used to have more sophisticated order options such as "Execute based on certain conditions". Most investors do not need this feature.

They require you to apply for trading options, after-hour trading, using margin and trading penny stocks. Gift appreciated stocks to your children who have a tax bracket lower than yours up to $15,000 of the current market value for each receiver ($30,000 per couple) in 2019. Gifting depreciated stocks is not recommended. Consult your tax lawyer or CPA.

Ensure all accounts have primary beneficiaries and secondary beneficiaries. I have a simple trust for my taxable account for myself and my spouse. Consult your lawyer for estate planning.

Fidelity offers CD ladders so they mature in different time frames. I prefer Fidelity rather than local banks as it saves me trips to the bank (to purchase and renew) by doing my purchasing CDs on-line. However, my state offers some tax deductions for the interests from local banks. The other advantage is the bank CDs can start right away.

Save some interest in the cash account. If you have the CASH account (FCASH), change it to Government Money Market fund FDRXX by clicking on the core account. Today I have to buy SPRXX that pays better dividends than FDRXX. Automatically SPRXX will be used when the core account is exhausted. Check the current information and dividends. SPRXX should be part of the choices.

My annuity has gained 4 times during decades. I do not recommend the use of an annuity, most of which have high commissions for the sales persons. My tax rate today is higher than during my work life. Compared to many other offers, Fidelity's annuity is better than the average.

The only negative I have found is their margin interest rates are quite high. If you use margin a lot, open a second account that has a low interest rate such as from Interactive Broker.

I transferred my appreciated stocks to my son's account as he is in lower tax bracket. The performance of my account was less while my son's increased. It may be correct, but it is not I want.

I use their two-factor log in for better security that I recommend you to use for all financial accounts if available.

Traders should use Fidelity's Active Trader Pro. Their low-cost ETFs are attractive.

My major credit card is with Fidelity that gives me 2% cash back. I have no relationship with Fidelity except being a retiree of Fidelity.

Link
Fidelity vs Vanguard. I believe Vanguard will improve to be competitive.
https://www.youtube.com/watch?v=tskh-QCCH-o

#Filler: Simple measures to reduce net security.
Do not click any links from unknown sources. Some seems to be ok but not.

"MalwareBytes", for checking viruses, is free for download (they do not pay me).

Personally I use a Chromebook for my financial transactions and a two-factor logon for my stock trading.

Filler: The most powerful word
I was deeply moved by the family members of the church victims forgiving the shooter. I wrote a brief post: "Forgive" is the most powerful word in every language and in every culture. I forgot it until I received a response from Jim.

"Tony,
Without even knowing it, you made the greatest comment I have seen on here--and it had nothing to do with investing. You mentioned somewhere that "Forgive" is the most powerful word in every language. Wow."

5   Covered calls

For basic descriptions on a covered call from Wikipedia, click here or enter (http://en.wikipedia.org/wiki/Covered_call) in your browser.

It is like collecting rent from the apartment you bought. The difference is that the renter has an option to buy the apartment at a preset time and price.

The rent is quite substantial if you do good planning. To start with, you want to buy stocks that have a market to sell. Usually they are large companies with high trading volumes.

Since one contract is for 100 shares of a stock, you cannot sell a covered call on 50 shares of a stock. On the other hand, when you have 1,000 stocks, the commission of 10 contracts would be more than the cost of 1 contract depending on your broker's schedule.

It is time consuming to keep track of the covered calls but it is well worth your time and effort. If the stock price exceeds the strike price of your covered call, you may want to buy the same shares back, so you would not miss any further appreciation of this stock.

However, if it is in a taxable account and you have a loss in a forced sell, do not buy it back otherwise the tax loss is not allowed (i.e. a wash sale) for the year as of 2016. When the contract expires, you may want to start another contract on the same stock if the stock has   not   been   sold.

Covered calls do have their disadvantages such as higher commission rates and sometimes forcing you to sell at a higher tax rate for short-term capital gains in taxable accounts. It is avoidable by using covered calls on stocks that are qualified for long-term capital gains. In addition, you need to buy them back when they increase in price beyond your strike price or lose its potential to appreciate further. Using another put could keep you from not losing any gains beyond the strike price. However, I prefer to use my time in more productive ways and this insurance is not cheap. One's opinion.

One company advertises their techniques using covered calls which could give their users 3 to 6% monthly returns. If you believe in this fantasy, you do not need this book. There is no free lunch.

My recent experience

I sold Netflix covered calls with the strike price about 2% higher and a 3% premium (from my memory) but the price shot up 12% higher in one day, so I was potentially losing 7% profit. However, it turned out to be a good experience as Netflix went downhill later (8/2012).

Normally I prefer to sell covered options for stocks with a quantity from 100 to 600 shares (i.e. 1 to 6 contracts) for the longest time (about 2-3 months). Some non-volatile and small stocks are not candidates to write covered calls on. Some stocks are not optionable. Typically high-tech stocks have a higher premium to be collected as their stock prices fluctuate more. The right stocks can generate 10% or even more a year in addition to the fluctuations of the stock prices.

In general, if I feel the market will be down for the period, I use covered calls especially for stocks holding over one year (unless I have short-term loss to offset any short-term gains) in taxable accounts. Watch out for any tax change that may affect your total return.

Recently I attended a sales pitch on a 3-day training course on a strategy for making 24% per year and it is quite possible especially with the S&P 500 returns about the same. I wish it were available to me 15 years ago. It seems to be too good to be true.

How to sell covered calls

First you need to open an account with your broker and apply to trade options including covered calls.

Check how your broker charges commissions. Ask how much they charge for one contract and 10 contracts of a stock.

The covered call is an agreement to sell the rights to the buyer of the stock at the strike price for a specific date range (a.k.a. expiration date). Typically options expire on Fridays.

You need to write covered calls on the stocks you already own. One contract is 100 shares of stocks. Check out the option chain to select the price, expiration period and the strike price. Normally, the strike price should be higher than the current market price. You may want to have an expiration date 2 weeks or longer. When the contract is expiring in a few days, the contract has little value and most likely the small 'rent' is not worth the risk and the commission.

When the covered call is sold, you receive the 'rent' immediately and any dividend during the 'rental' period.

When the option is 'called' due to a price rise above the strike price, your stock will be sold and you will have to pay the regular commission.

At this point, evaluate the stock to check whether you want to buy it back. If the stock surges, you may have to pay a higher price – thus losing the extra appreciation. In addition, you may have to pay a higher capital gains tax if it is held less than the required period for long-term capital gains in a taxable account.

Note. Notice that some stocks are not optionable and/or not practical to write options on. Most brokers charge a flat rate for the first contract (such as $7) and an incremental fee for each additional contract. Shop around as the fees vary if you write a lot of covered calls.

The best stocks for covered calls are large US companies with a large average volume. The option (a.k.a. the 'rent') pays better for volatile companies such as high-tech companies. From my rough estimates for illustration purposes, the annualized return on covered calls for AAPL is 25% and C is 12% after commission.

#Filler: Double standard
We set up our standard in everything and the entire world has to follow our standard. Shooting citizens at each other, separating children from the illegals, and police brutality are fine according to our standard.

6   Selling short

This article describes the advantages, disadvantages and how to avoid the pitfalls in selling short. Next we describe the procedures.

Advantages

You consider short selling (same as shorting) when you believe the stock and / or the market is going down. It is easier to make money via selling short than buying stocks especially in a plunging market. Many mutual funds cannot short stocks, and consequently they spend less time in searching for poor companies. The other factor is psychology: Most retail investors do not want to sell losers.

You should start paper trading. Commit a small amount of money gradually when you have proved to yourself your strategy (i.e. what and when to short sell, and exit) is profitable. Consult your financial advisor first and read my Disclaimer under Introduction.

Beginners should try to short the sectors by buying contra ETFs. The major advantages are: 1. Less volatile, 2. Can trade in retirement accounts (some brokers have some restrictions), 3. Do not lose more than your initial trade position, and 4. Fees and dividends are handled for you. Short selling stocks is risker but more profitable than a group stocks in ETFs.

Disadvantages and some suggestions

- Short stocks when the market is plunging and limit your shorting positions when the market is rising. The market rises more than falls, and hence be careful. However, when the market plunges, it is fast and steep.

- Could lose more than 100% of the investment.
  Actually, in theory, there is no limit. If the price of the shorted stock rises by 10 times, the loss is well over 10 times the money of the short position. The 2015 example was Weight Watchers. The price boosted up by more than 170% when Oprah took out a position on them. Fundamentally this stock was not sound and it should be shorted. No stock pickers without insider information (that is illegal) can predict that. Use stops to protect

your trade (i.e. cover your short when you lose a percent specified by you).

- Need to pay dividends and interest for the shorted stock. The higher the dividend rate for the stock, the more you have to pay. Investors should avoid high-dividend stocks when shorting unless the expected shorting period is only brief.

  In addition, you need to pay interest for 'borrowing' the stocks to sell. Brokers charge interest rates differently and it could be huge savings to shop around if you short stocks a lot.

- Need both fundamental and technical analyses. From my experience, technical analysis is more important than fundamentals in shorting especially for short holding periods.

- If shorting a stock is successful and closed within a year, the gain is usually subjected to the short-term capital gains taxes which are typically higher than the long-term capital gains taxes. Check the current tax laws and consult your tax lawyer.

- Not all of the stocks can be shorted. Your broker may not have the stock you want to short. It is also possible that your broker can close out your short positions for various reasons; they need to protect their 'loans' to you. Check the margin status with your broker.

- Selling short is not allowed in retirement accounts as of 2020. However, you can buy contra ETFs for a group of stocks to bet against the market or a specific sector, but not on a specific stock in retirement accounts.

- The following sectors are riskier: the drug, mine, bank (unless you know the quality of their mortgages) and insurance sectors. An approval of a drug could drive the stock price up by more than 25% in one day. The same for earnings announcements. It could drive the stock more than 10% in either direction.

- Your screens may find many stocks in bio tech companies. These companies especially with a market cap of less than 1B may have the worst fundamentals. However, when they have a new discovery, the stock prices could rocket. Do not short them when insiders are buying (Insider Transaction in Finviz.com) and high SMA-20% or SMA-50% (from Finviz.com).

- There is no perfect timing. Some stocks fluctuate a lot with no rational reasons, or the prices are driven by institutional investors. Some stocks could be manipulated. The shorted stocks could move up for a long time until they finally crash. Hence, do not short against a rising stock, a sector or a market. When the market is rising, shorting a rising stock in a rising sector is dangerous, and the opposite could be profitable for shorting.

- The best time to short is when the market is plunging. At that time, the best sectors to short are those sectors that are plunging. Hence, find the worst stocks in a worst sector in a plunging market.

- A bad company could be acquired by another company due to a good buy; it could boost its stock price. It is same when the major problem of a company has been fixed.

- Use mental stops (i.e. set a price you can afford to lose and when it reaches the specific price, place a market trade to exit the shorted shares. You do not want to make 5% several times and lose 50% in one trade.

- You may not want to short companies that are fundamentally unsound but with a good momentum (i.e. trending up). They may have good prospects such as improved profit, being turned around, settling a lawsuit and/ or new products are being legalized and/or approved. If you do, then use mental stops to protect your trades.

- Never short sell the stocks that are rising even they are not fundamentally sound such as FAANG in 2015 to 2020. Tesla has gained many times and you have to pay the gains, not limited to your short position.

- I have turned some short selling candidates into buying due to the high insiders' buying and/or high short squeeze potential.

- Watch out for short squeezes when the short percentage approaches over 25%. In a nut shell, the stock is running out of shares to be shorted. As a result, it would rise in price especially on any good news. As of 8/2015, I expect short squeeze for PPC and SAFM (CALM in 12/2015) for the following reasons:

  1   The shorting has no bases. It is most likely from one or two hedge funds.
  2   Fundamentally sound.
  3   Beef will be replaced by a lot of healthier and cheaper chicken if not already, esp. during the drought in California.
  4   In Hong Kong for example, they do not allow live chickens imported from China during the bird flu breakout, but they did allow frozen chicken from the USA if there was no political game going on.

What to buy & how

Refer to the chapter on screening short candidates. If Fidelity's Equity Summary Score for the stock is below 4, it is a short candidate.

The following are my suggestions on shorting stocks that have the potential to go down. Basically these stocks are both fundamentally unsound and technically unsound. Many sites (some require paid subscriptions) provide a composite grade for fundamentals and technical. Finviz.com. a free financial site, does provide most of these metrics and many of them are discussed here. If you do not hold the shorts for a long period, technical (the trend) parameters are more important. Parameters for short candidates are:

- Fundamentals

  - The price is more than four times the book value.
  - EY (= 1 / (P/E) is negative. Negative PEG is another consideration.
  - High debts (Debt/Equity > .5) except for industries that require high debts such as utilities.
  - Insiders are unloading their company's stocks. They do this for many reasons. But, when they are buying, do not short the stock as they may know some positive events that we do not know.

- Bad intangibles such as losing market share and/or a major lawsuit(s) is pending.
  Read articles on the company from Finviz, Fidelity, Seeking Alpha, etc.
- Do not short stocks that are on their uptrend. It includes the current marijuana stocks that most have no fundamental values and/or historical data.
- Do not short small stocks with a small market cap or float. I usually short stocks with a market cap or float > 200M (100M for riskier investors). Use higher values for conservative investors.

  The stocks with small floats may be controlled by the owners; if they do not sell, the stocks available to trade will be limited. Another indicator is the Avg. Daily Vol. Personally it should be 100 times higher than my bet.

- Technical metrics:

  - Be careful on stocks that have plunged more than 15% recently (Finviz's last quarter performance gives us some hint). It could mean the bottom has been reached.
  - Overbought (RSI(14) > 65). There may be a reason, so it is only a secondary consideration. Most stocks to be shorted may have RSI(14) less than 30.
  - The momentum metrics such as SMA-20 and SMA-50 are important too. SMA-20% and SMA-50% from Finviz.com should be negative (i.e. trending downwards).
  - Some sites especially the paid sites may give you a momentum grade. Select the stocks with a bad momentum grade (a.k.a. timing grade). However, if it is the lowest grade, be careful, as it has nowhere to go but up.

Trading considerations
- Do not trade in the first hour (first half hour for me) as there may have new developments overnight.
- I use subscription services. I do not trade on Monday or the day after a holiday, as the data is at least one day late.
- Your broker may limit your short trade (limited order) to be valid for the day; check this with your broker.
- Your broker may need to approve whether you can short stocks based on your experiences.

- When you sell short and are using limit orders, enter a sell price higher than the last trade price just like selling a stock.
- Close the short position when your trade loses a pre-defined percentage which depends on your personal tolerance.
- Put Option is similar to shorting a company. It is not for beginners.

Margin

Margin should not be used extensively. It is expensive and most brokers try every trick they can to squeeze profits from all transactions to subsidize their low-commission incomes. Usually you can borrow up to 40% of your current position and the rules and the margin rates vary among brokers.

Many investors had losses during the last two market plunges. However, many including myself had made a killing in 2003 and 2009 using margin. I use it for the following reasons.

- For convenience in placing buy orders that exceed my cash position in my taxable accounts.
- I can pay back my outstanding margin loans from my home equity loan (check the current tax laws) as it is far, far lower than my broker's margin interest rates. However, I do not recommend this for conservative investors.

Random case

- As of 7/2013, shorting Amazon, Netflix and Tesla as a group was not beneficial. It is best to stay away from shorting, except during the plunging (from peak to bottom) in the market cycle.
- Did you watch 60 minutes on Lumber Liquidators in 2015? That's how you do shorting. Find out why the company boosts its profit and stock price in such a short period. If it has been proven to be fishy, place a short position. However, when the news becomes public, it could be too late for us to act.

Links & Articles
Introduction
https://www.youtube.com/watch?v=oMnmTV5HF5Y&list=WL&index=3&t=605s
Fidelity Video: Selling short.https://www.fidelity.com/learning-center/trading/selling-short-video

7   Tax avoidance

Tax avoidance is a good way to save some money legally. Tax laws change all the time. Check Wikipedia on current investment taxes. Consult your tax lawyer as my knowledge in taxes is limited, and the tax laws are always changing.

In general for Federal returns on your taxable accounts (as opposed to IRA, Roth IRA, IRA-Rollover and 401K), you have to pay taxes on dividends either at the ordinary income rate or at a qualified rate which is usually lower. If the stock that was held longer than a year, you pay long-term capital tax (max. 20%). The short-term capital tax rate at the ordinary income rate up to 37%. In addition, you may have to pay state and local taxes. Currently, you can offset $3,000 or up to your total losses from your regular income.

Do not implement what I did as tax laws change frequently and every one's situation is different. Here is what I did and I hope it will be applicable to you.

- Sold most profitable stocks that I held more than a year in taxable accounts in 2011 to qualify for long-term capital gains. Usually they have more favorable tax treatments than the short-term capital gains, which are treated as ordinary income. I bought some back. I maintained a 15% tax bracket, so the tax bill from Uncle Sam is virtually 0 (not exactly due to more tax on social security and Medicare as a result of the trades). I still had to pay state tax. As a retiree, I can control my income.

- Converted part of my Rollover IRA to Roth in 2012 and 2013. I paid taxes today. However, the Roth conversion gives me tax-free appreciation for the future trades in this account and it will lower taxes and my minimum withdrawal requirement in the future. Check whether it is still available.

- The taxes from dividends in the retirement accounts are deferred but eventually they will be treated as regular income when they are withdrawn. Very few people have higher income during their retirement. If you are the lucky few due to the successful investing in your retirement accounts, you may end up with a higher tax bracket during your retirement, particularly when you are forced to withdraw at age 70 ½.

- Gifted some appreciated stocks to my children. The current price of the gifted stock is used in calculating the total cost allowed, not the price you paid for them. I prefer the value stocks that have potential for long-term appreciation. It is good for them and not good for Uncle Sam. You can gift up to $15,000 (in 2019) for each spouse to each child without paying any Federal tax. For a family of four, you and your spouse can gift up to $60,000 (= 15,000 * 4) a year.

  The link: https://www.irs.gov/businesses/small-businesses-self-employed/frequently-asked-questions-on-gift-taxes

The cost basis of the transferred stock is quite complicated. Check out the current tax law. The cost basis of the appreciated stocks are carried to the receiver, so it would lower your capital taxes as most of us are in higher tax brackets than our children.

From my experience, the cost basis of the depreciated stocks after the transfer is the market price on the transfer day as of 2016. I do not understand it enough to comment but just to tell you what I have experienced. I tried to offset my son's unexpected short-term capital gain by transferring a losing stock and that does not work.

- My lawyer set up trusts for me including my house. They will avoid probate hopefully. From the current tax law (as of 2016), the cost basis of your stocks will be stepped up or down to the stock prices on that day you pass away. Ask your heirs to keep a business paper for the stock prices or tell your brokers to adjust the cost basis on the day you pass away. Of course, you have to tell your heirs now to take care of these tasks. Again, ask your tax lawyer for details.

Make sure you specify the beneficiaries in your and your spouse's accounts to avoid probate. Check your local state laws. Some states take more than a year to finish the probate process for a house. As of 2014, my state (Mass.) has an exemption of 1 million, not portable to your spouse, and they calculate the entire estate when it exceeds the exemption. There is no estate tax if my estate is a million dollar. I have to pay a rate on

1,000,001 if it just exceeds it by one dollar. That's why we should move 30 miles north to New Hampshire.

I estimate that it takes about three years for the average estate to be distributed. You want to cut down the duration by having a will to start with, so you do not want to pay extra for your lawyer.

- At age 70 ½ (as of 2016), you are required to withdraw them in a schedule and it could put you in higher tax bracket. Roth withdrawal is not counted in the mandatory withdrawal for a person's lifetime as of 2016.

- Roth IRA if qualified could be the best deal for most. However, you have to use after-tax money to fund your Roth IRA.

- I simulate my next year via my tax preparation software and adjust my income accordingly.

- Most oil partnerships and many MLPs require you to file special tax forms for non-retirement accounts in 2017. I avoided most of them as my time is limited. Some ETFs require you to file the complicated K-1 (vs 1099) in your tax return. You can find this requirement in ETFdb.com. You can avoid them by not buying these ETFs; I prefer to buy them in my non-taxable accounts (i.e. retirement accounts). Usually the taxes on these dividends are lowered as they are treated the return of investment after depreciation.

- Avoid wash sales in your taxable accounts
  http://en.wikipedia.org/wiki/Wash_sale

You cannot claim the loss for the year if you buy back the stock within 30 days. Before I buy, I check whether I sold this loser in the last 30 days. Before I sell a loser, I check whether I bought it in the last 30 days.

I placed one order to sell a loser at a higher price and another one to buy it back at a lower price. When there is a big swing in price for that stock, both orders were executed within 30 days. I cannot claim the loss of the sold stock for that year. However, the loss can be adjusted to the cost basis of the newly-acquired stock as of 2013.

There are many ways to avoid it. Try not to buy it back within 30 days (check the current regulation) and this is the best way. IRS has more restrictions and it is better not to push it to the limit. Buy a similar stock in the same sector. Buy it in your children's account. Again, check the current tax laws.

Afterthoughts

- Tax audit signs.
  http://money.cnn.com/gallery/pf/taxes/2014/03/14/tax-audit/index.html?iid=HP_LN
  Your business would be treated as a hobby if you do not have a profit in three out of the last five years. Day traders and businesses can deduct all the trading expenses. Some form an investing company in some Caribbean island to avoid paying taxes. Again check the current tax laws.

- As of 2013, the dividend tax is at 20% max. Do not believe it is no tax in tax-deferred accounts. When you withdraw, it will be treated as a regular income and it can be as high as almost 40% (as of 2013). Your dividend tax rate depends on your income.

- When you trade 5 times or more a week, investigate whether you're eligible to trade as a business by the current tax rule. A business allows its owner to deduct business expenses.

- Fidelity: Investment tax.
  https://www.fidelity.com/learning-center/mutual-funds/tax-implications-bond-funds

  ETF Taxes on Foreign Stocks:
  http://seekingalpha.com/article/2491465-foreign-withholding-taxes-in-international-equity-etfs

Links
Tax Avoidance:
http://en.wikipedia.org/wiki/Tax_avoidance
Tax Law:
http://en.wikipedia.org/wiki/Income_tax_%28U.S.%29

Epilogue

After my early retirement, I have been spending most of my time in investing, running thousands of simulation and reading over one hundred books in investing. Starting from 2000, I have been doing extraordinary good. I comment in financial blogs and save the good ones in my own blog, so I can refer them later on. After several years, I have enough information to write a book.

At first, I want to write a book for one reader only: Me. My children have better things to do than investing. I do not need to keep my 'secrets' for them. That's why I publish this book. From the pre-release version, it had been doing better than my expectation. It has been very rewarding, when my readers tell me how much they enjoy and benefit from this book.

A good pointer can make you thousands of dollars, and a bad or misinterpreted one can do the opposite. Always do paper testing on any strategy and / or idea before you commit real money on it. Start your strategy with cash in small increments until you have more confidence.

I've received a lot of good responses and thanks. The 2nd Edition incorporates a lot of your feedbacks and updates. Some complaints are not valid though.

- The primary objective of this book is helping you make money, not improving your English skill. Based on the techniques here, I have been profitable.

- As described in Introduction, charts and tables can be displayed in the full size of your reader by selecting it. I also provide links to the more important charts so you can display them on the large screen of your PC.

- The predictability of all metrics should be monitored and the scoring system should be modified accordingly.

If you believe this book is beneficial, please comment in amazon.com or similar sites.
https://www.amazon.com/dp/B015KQJ84W

Appendix 1 – All my books

- Complete the Art of Investing (highly recommended combining most of my books on investing). The Kindle version has over 850 pages (6*9), about 3 times the size of an investing book.
- Sector Rotation: 21 Strategies and another book Shorting (highly recommended for short-term investors) have more specific chapters on the topic and share many articles with "Complete the art of investing".
- Best stocks for 2022 (avail after Dec. 15, 2021).
- "Nuclear War with China".
- Books for today's market: Profit from Coming Market Crash.
- The following books are in a series: Finding Profitable Stocks, Market Timing and Scoring Stocks. Alternate books: Using Fidelity and Using Finviz.
- Books on strategies: "Profit from bull, bear and sideways markets" (Rotation + Momentum + ETF Rotation + trend following), Trading System (similar to printed version of Complete), Swing (Rotation + Momentum), ETF Rotation for Couch Potatoes, Momentum, SuperStocks, Dividend, Penny & Micro Stock, and Retiree.
- Books for advance beginners: Be an expert (highly recommended), Introduce, Investing for Beginners, Beat Fund Managers, Profit via ETFs, Buffett, Ideas, Conservative and Top-Down.
- Miscellaneous: Lessons in Investing. Investing Strategies. Buy Low and Sell High. Buy High and sell Higher. Buffettology. Technical Analysis. Trading Stocks.
- Concise Editions and Introduction Editions are available at very low prices and are competitive with books of similar sizes (50 pages) and prices ($3 range).

Most books have paperbacks. Links and offers are subject to change without notice.

Best stocks to buy for 2022 (avail. after Dec. 15, 21)

We care about performance only. Not considering dividends and fees, my last three books in this series have beaten the SPY (the market to most) by **110%, 71% and 25%** from the publish date to 07/01/2021.

Book	Stocks	Return	Ann.	Beat SPY by
Best Book for 2021 2nd Edition	10	20%	52%	110%
Best Book for 2021	4	29%	52%	71%

Best Book to Buy from Aug, 2020	14	42%	45%	25%
Avg.	9	31%	50%	69%

Appendix 2 – Complete the Art of Investing

Instead of buying 16 books, why not buy one book (Complete the Art of Investing) consisting of 16 books? Besides saving money and your digital shelve space, it gives you quick reference and concentration on the topic you're currently interested in. It covers most investing topics in investing excluding speculative investing such as currency trading and day trading.

The Kindle version has about 850 pages (6*9), about the size of three books of average size. With the cost of $10 and at least 850 investing ideas, it is about one cent per idea. Most other books have only a few ideas in the entire book

The 16 books

This book "Complete Art of Investing" is divided into 16 books as follows. Click for the link to the book described in Amazon.com. I squeezed more than 3,000 pages into 850 pages by eliminating duplicated information such as evaluating stocks.

Book No.	Amazon.com
1	Simple techniques
2	Finding Stocks
3	Evaluating Stocks
4	Scoring Stocks
5	Trading Stocks
6	Market Timing
7	Strategies
8	Sector Rotation
9	Insider Trading
10	Penny Stocks & Micro Cap
11	Momentum Investing
12	Dividend Investing
13	Technical Analysis
14	Investing Ideas
15	The Economy
16	Buffettology

The book links are subject to change without notice.

"How to be a billionaire" is for beginners and couch potatoes, who can use the advanced features of this book in the simplest and less time-consuming techniques. Most advance users can skip this section unless they want to use some of the short cuts described.

We start with the basic books Finding Stocks, Evaluate Stocks, Trading Stocks and Market Timing. You can select and start with one of the many styles and strategies in investing such as swing trading and top-down strategy. Many tools are described in other books such as ETFs, technical analysis, covered calls and trading plan.

Many books start with "Why" to lure you to read more and are followed by "How" and then the theory behind the book.
If the book you're reading is beneficial to you, imagine how it would with 850 pages.

Most readers' comments are on "Debunk the Myths in Investing", which this book is originally based on. As of 2018, I did not know any of the commentators on my books.

"I skipped ahead to his chapter book 14 (of "Complete the Art of Investing"), Investment Advice just to get a feel of his writing style. His research is phenomenal and doesn't overwhelm with big words or catchy "sales-like" tactics.

I truly believe this ordinary man, Mr. Tony Pow, has a gift of explaining his experience as an investor without the bull crap of trying to make you buy his stuff. He seemingly just wants to share his knowledge, tips, and clarity of definitions for the kind of folks like me who want to understand something FIRST before jumping in with emotions of trying to make a boat load of money. I like the technical analysis side he brings.

Mr. Tony Pow talks about hidden gems in his book; well....quite frankly, he is a hidden gem. Thank you and I will also post my comments about this author to my Facebook page!" – JB on this book.

"Excellent book, recommend to all investors... great knowledge. It has fine-tuned my investing strategies... Your book is hard to set aside, as I read it all the time learning good techniques and analysis of stocks, ETF... Since I purchased your book in March, I have underlined, highlighted and placed tabs on top of pages for quick reference." – Aileron on this book.

"Tony, I just finished reading your 2nd edition. It's my pleasure to report that I found it most interesting. You're welcome to use this blurb if you like:

Debunk the Myths in Investing is an all-encompassing look at not only the most salient factors influencing markets and investors, but also a from-the-trenches look at many of the misconceptions and mistakes too many investors make. Reading this book may save not only time and aggravation but money as well!"

Joseph Shaefer, CEO, Stanford Wealth Management LLC.

"Tony, Great work!" from James and Chris, who are portfolio managers.

"'Debunk the Myths in Investing' is a comprehensive book on investing that deals with many aspects of this tense profession in which with a lot of knowledge and a bit of luck (or vice versa) one can greatly benefit...

Therefore 'Debunk the Myths in Investing' is an interesting book that on its 500 pages offer a lot of knowledge related to investing world and many practical advice, so I can recommend its reading if you're interested in this topic."
- Denis Vukosav, Top 500 Reviewers at Amazon.com.

"490 pages (Debunk) of a genius's ranting and hypothesis with various theories throughout, written light-heartedly with ample doses of humor...Yes, the myth of not being able to profitably time the market is BUSTED...

One might ask... Why is he giving away the results of his hard-earned research for only $20? He states that his children are not interested in investing and wants to share his efforts with the world." - Abe Agoda.

"Excellent book, recommend to all investors... great knowledge. It has fine-tuned my investing strategies... Your book is hard to set aside, as I read it all the time learning good techniques and analysis of stocks, ETF... Since I purchased your book in March, I have underlined, highlighted and placed tabs on top of pages for quick reference." - Aileron on this book.

"Great stuff, Tony. It's great to meet experienced traders such as yourself. I had a browse through the book and think your method is a little more refined than mine."

"Your strategy is very rules based and solid. I sometimes envy people who have developed something like this."

Making 50% in one month
I claim to have the best one-month performance ever for recommending 8 or more stocks without using options and leverage. My following return is 57% in a month or 621% annualized. They are slightly different as I calculated the average from the averages of three different accounts. The average buy date is 12/26/18 and the "current date" is 01/28/19.
The performance may not be repeated. I will use the same screen for the coming years and even the expected 10% (or 120% annualized) is very good.

I used the same screen for searching stock candidates. I spent a total of about 20 hours from Dec. 15, 2018 to Jan. 5, 2019.

Stock	Buy Price	Sold or Current Price	Buy date	Sold or Current date	Profit %	Profit % Ann.	Status
CHK	2.13	2.99	01/03/09	01/18/19	40%	982%	Sold
MNK	16.41	21.45	01/03/19	01/25/19	31%	510%	Sold
MNK	16.43	21.45	01/03/19	01/25/19	31%	507%	Sold
NNBR	5.68	8.58	12/26/18	01/28/19	51%	565%	
NNBR	5.72	8.58	12/26/18	01/28/19	66%	727%	
ESTE	4.35	6.45	12/26/18	01/18/19	48%	766%	Sold
LCI	4.61	8.29	12/21/18	01/28/19	80%	767%	
MDR	8.01	9.13	01/08/19	01/28/19	14%	255%	
YRCW	3.29	5.78	12/21/18	01/28/19	76%	727%	
YRCW	3.26	5.78	12/21/18	01/28/19	77%	742%	
ASRT	3.56	4.18	12/26/18	01/28/19	17%	193%	
UTCC	7.13	11.00	12/26/18	01/28/19	54%	600%	
YRCW	2.92	5.78	12/26/18	01/28/19	98%	1083%	

Best one-year return
I claim to have the best-performed article in Seeking Alpha history, an investing site, for recommending 15 or more stocks in one year after the publish date without using options and leverage.

https://seekingalpha.com/article/1095671-amazing-returns-velti-alcatel-lucent-alpha-natural-resources

Your choice
"Complete the art of investing" should be your first choice. If you are short-term trading, I recommend "Sector Rotation: 21 Strategies" and "Shorting Stocks /ETFs". These 3 books together with "Using Fidelity" share many articles.

My recommended stocks can be found in my "Best stocks" series. It would be published on Dec. 15 – it is not a promise. So far, this book and "Sector Rotation: 21 Strategies" are my best sellers. All info are subject to change without notice.

Sector Rotation: 21 Strategies

In addition, as of 5/2020 I bet that no author besides me made **over 4 times** using sector rotation starting the amount more than his yearly salary then.

- On 5/26/2020, I searched for "Sector Rotation" under Amazon's Book. They are listed in the same order except my book Sector Rotation: 21 Strategies.

Book	Date	Size[1]	Kindle $[1]	Hard $
Sector Rotation: 21 Strategies	**05/2020**	**425**	**$9.95**	$24.95
Super Sectors	09/2010	289	$26.39	$49.95
Dual Momentum Investing	11/2014	240	$40.40	$42.20
Sector Investing	05/1996	260		$29.94
Sector Trading Strategies	08/2007	164	$26.39	$16.66
The Sector Strategist	03/2012	225	$26.39	$44.96
ETF Rotation	10/2012	125	**$9.95**	**$14.99**
Optimal... Sector Rotation	07/2015	80		$44.07

[1] From Amazon on size and prices as of 5/25/2020. Last update is 09/2021.

My book won in all categories except the price for hard copy in one. However, my book won as the lowest cost per page by a wide margin.

- I have **21** strategies in sector rotation while most books have only one. It ranges from simple rotation of a stock ETF and cash for beginners to many advanced strategies for experts. Most other books have one or two strategies.

- Andrew, a contributor on Sector Rotation article at Seeking Alpha, said, "Great stuff, Tony. It's great to meet experienced traders such as yourself. I had a browse through the book and think your method is a little more refined than mine."

Appendix 3 - Our window to the investing world

The paperback version of this chapter can be found in the following link.
http://ebmyth.blogspot.com/2013/11/web-sites.html

- **General**
  Wikipedia / Investopedia /Yahoo!Finance / MarketWatch / Cnnfn / Morningstar /CNBC / Bloomberg / WSJ / Barron's / Motley Fool / TheStreet
- **Evaluate stocks**
  Finviz / SeekingAlpha / MSN Money / Zacks / Daily Finance / ADR / Fidelity / BlueChipGrowth / Earnings Impact / OpenInsider / NYSE / NASDAQ / SEC / SEC for 10K and 10Q (quarterly) reports required to file for listed stocks in major exchanges.
- **Charts**
  BigCharts / FreeStockCharts / StockCharts /
- **Screens**
  Yahoo!Finance / Finviz / CNBC / Morningstar /
- **Besides stocks**
  123Jump / Hoover's Online / FINRA Bond Market Data / REIT / Commodity Futures / Option Industry
- **Vendors**
  AAII / Zacks / IBD / GuruFocus / Vector Vest / Fidelity / Interactive Brokers / Merrill Lynch /
- **Economy.**
  Econday / EcoconStats / Federal Reserve / Economist /
- **Misc.**
  Dow Jones Indices / Russell / Wilshire / IRS / Wikinvest / ETF Database / ETF Trends / Nolo (estate planning) / AARP /

Appendix 4 - ETFs / Mutual Funds

What is an ETF

ETFs have basic differences from mutual funds: 1. Lower management expenses, 2. Trade ETFs same as stocks, and 3. Usually more diversified but not selective than the related mutual funds such as NOBL vs FRDPX.

The major classifications of ETFs are 1. Simulating an index such as SPY, QQQ and DIA, 2. Simulating a sector such as XLE and SOXX, 3. Simulating an asset class such as GLD and SLV, 4. Simulating a country or a group of countries such as EWC and FXI, 5. Managed by a manager(s) such as ARKK, 6. Betting a market or sector to go down such as SH and PSQ, and 7. Leveraged (not recommended for beginners).

Fidelity: Index ETFs (https://www.fidelity.com/etfs/overview).

Wikipedia on ETF (http://en.wikipedia.org/wiki/Exchange-traded_fund).

List of ETFs

ETF Bloomberg
http://www.bloomberg.com/markets/etfs/
ETF data base
http://etfdb.com/
ETF Trends
http://www.etftrends.com/
A list of ETFs. Seeking Alpha.
(http://etf.stock-encyclopedia.com/category/)

Fidelity's commission-free ETFs. Check current offerings and whether they are still commission-free.
(https://www.fidelity.com/etfs/ishares)

Fidelity Annuity funds with performance data.

http://fundresearch.fidelity.com/annuities/category-performance-annual-total-returns-quarterly/FPRAI?refann=005

A list of contra ETFs (or bear ETFs)
http://www.tradermike.net/inverse-short-etfs-bearish-etf-funds/

Misc.: ETFGuide, ETFReplay (highly recommended).

Other resources
Your broker should have a lot of information on ETFs and many offer commission-free ETFs.

Most subscription services offer research on ETFs. IBD has a strategy dedicated to ETFs and so does AAII to name a couple. Seeking Alpha has extensive resources for ETF including an ETF screener and investing ideas.

Not all ETFs are created equal
Check their performances and their expenses.

Small but well-performing ETFs
Here is a list.
http://finance.yahoo.com/news/small-etfs-pack-big-punch-195430875.html

Guggenheim Spin-Off ETF (CSD) looks interesting. The ETF tracks corporate spinoffs. It has beaten SPY for a long time; check the current performance. Not a recommendation.

When not to use ETFs
I prefer sector mutual funds in some industries but you need to do extensive research. They are drug industry, banks, miners and insurers.

Half ETF
Taking out half of the stocks that score below the average in an index ETF could beat the same full ETF itself. I call it HETF (half the ETF). You heard it here first.

To illustrate, sort the expected P/E (not including stocks with negative earnings) in ascending order and only include the stocks on the first half. Add more fundamental metrics. It will take a few minutes.

Disadvantages of ETFs
- When you have two stocks in a sector ETF one good one and one bad one, the ETF treats them the same. Stock pickers would buy the one that has a better appreciation potential.
- The return is better than the actual return due to stock rotation. To illustrate this, on August 29, 2012, SHLD was replaced by LYB in a sector fund. SHLD was down by 4% and LYB was up by 4% primarily due to the switch. Unless you sell and buy at the right time (which is impossible), your return would not match the ETF's returns due to the replacement.
- Ensure the performance matches the corresponding index, but will most likely not include dividends.

Advantages of ETFs
- We have demonstrated that you can beat the market by using market timing. Between 2000 and Nov., 2013, you only exit and reenter the market 3 times and the result is astonishing.
- It is easy to rotate a sector vs. buying/selling all of the stocks in this sector. It makes sector rotation the same as trading a stock.
- The risk is spread out and your portfolio is diversified especially for a market ETF or buying three or more ETFs in different sectors.
- Eliminate the time in researching stocks.

Leveraged ETFs
I do not recommend them. Some are 2x, 3x and even higher. They're too risky. However, when you are very sure or your tested strategy has very low drawdown, you may want to use them to improve performance. I recommend skipping all leveraged ETFs.

My basic ETF tables

I use a list of selected ETFs and commission-free (check the details) ETFs from Fidelity for my purpose. I include some mutual funds in Fidelity's annuity. Some of these may be interesting to you. I use ETFs for sector rotation and parking my cash when the market is favorable and I do not have stocks that I want to buy.

ETFs and funds come and go. Some ideas and classifications are my own interpretation.

Table by market cap:

Category	ETF	Fidelity ETF	Mutual Funds	Fidelity's Annuity	Contra ETF
Size:					
Large Cap	DIA		See Blend		DOG
	SPY				SH
	QQQ	ONEQ			PSQ
	RYH				
Blend	IWD	IVV	BEQGX		
Growth	SPYG	IVW	FBGRX		
Value	SPYV		DOGGX		
Dividend	NOBL	DVY	FRDPX		
	VYM				
Mid Cap				FNBSC	MYY
Blend	MDY	JJH	VSEQX		
Growth		IJK	STDIX		
			BPTRX		
Value		IJJ	FSMVX		
Small Cap				FPRGC	SBB
Blend	IWM	IJR	HDPSX		
Growth		IJT	PRDSX		
Value		IJS	SKSEX		
Micro	IWC				
Multi					
Blend			VDEOX		
Growth			VHCOX		
Value			TCLCX		
Bond					
Long Term (20)	VLV		BTTTX		TBF
Mid Term (7 – 10)	VCIT		FSTGX		
Short Term (1 – 3 yrs.)	VCSH		THOPX		
Total	BOND		PONDX		
Corp Invest Grade	VCIT		NTHEX		
High Yield (junk)	PHB		SPHIX		
Muni	MUB		Check state		

Special situation					
Buy back	PKW				

Table by sectors:

Sector	ETF	Fidelity ETF	Mutual Funds	Fidelity's Annuity
Banking[1]			FSRBK	
Regional	IAT			
Bio Tech	IBB		FBIOX	
	XBI		Large	
Consumer Dis.	XLY	FDIS	FSCPX	FVHAC
Consumer Staple	XLP	FSTA	FDFAX	FCSAC
Finance	KIE	FNCL	FIDSX	FONNC
	IYF			
Energy	XLE	FENY	FSENX	FJLLC
Energy Service			FSESX	
Gold	GLD		FSAGX	
Gold Miner	GDX		VGPMX	
Health Care	IYH	FHLC	FSPHX	FPDRC
	VHT		VGHCX	
House Builder	ITB		FSHOX	
	ITB		Perform	
Industrial	IYJ	FIDU	FCYIX	FBALC
Material	VAW	FMAT	FSDPX	
	IYM			
Oil	USO			
Oil Service	OIH		FSESX	
Oil Exploration	XOP			
Real Estate	VNQ		FRIFX	FFWLC
REIT	VNQ			
Retail	RTH		FSRPX	
	XRT			
Regional bank	KRE		FSRBX	
Semi Conduct	SMH			
Software	XSW		FSCSX	
	IGV			
Technology	XLK	FTEC	FSPTX	FYENC

	FDN		FBSOX	
			ROGSX	
Telecomm.	VOX	FCOM	FSTCX	FVTAC
Transport	XTN			
	IYT			
Utilities	XLU	FUTY	FSUTX	FKMSC
Wireless			FWRLX	

Footnote. [1] Also check Finance.

Table by countries outside the USA:

Country	ETF	Fidelity ETF	Mutual Funds	Fidelity's Annuity
Australia	EWA			
Brazil	EWZ			
Canada	EWC		FICDX	
China	FXI		FHKCX	
EAFE	EFA			
Emerging	VWO		FEMEX	FEMAC
Europe	VGK		FIEUX	
Global	KXI		PGVFX	
Greece	GREK			
India	INDY		MINDX	
Indonesia	EIDO			
Latin America	ILF		FLATX	
Nordic			FNORX	
Hong Kong	EWH			
Japan	EWJ		FJPNX	
S. Africa	EZA			
S. Korea	EWY		MAKOX	
Singapore	EWS			
Taiwan	EWT			
	TUR			
United Kingdom	EWU			
Foreign:				
Combination	1	2	3	4
Intern. Div.	IDV	DWX		
Small Cap	SCZ	GWX		
Value	EFV			
Europe	VGK			

Rotate four ETFs

We can beat the market by rotating one ETF that represents the market such as SPY and cash (or short-term bond ETF) via market timing.

During a market uptrend, rotating the following four ETFs could be more profitable. Be warned that a short-term capital gain in taxable accounts is not treated as favorably as the long-term capital gain; check current tax laws.

The allocation percentages depend on your individual risk tolerance. You can use indexed mutual funds. Compare their expenses and restrictions. Some mutual funds charge you if you withdraw within a specific time period.

Select the best performer of last month (from Seeking Alpha, cnnFn, or the ETF/mutual fund site). Add a contra ETF such as SH to take advantage of a falling market for more aggressive investors. Add sector ETFs to the four ETFs such as XLY, XLP, XLE, XLF, XLU, IYW, XHB, IYM, OIL and XLU to expand your selection.

ETFs	Money Market	US	International	Bond
Fidelity		Spartan Total Market	Spartan Global Market	Spartan US Bond
Vanguard		Total Stock Market	Total International Market	Total Bond Market
My choice	Fidelity	SPY	Vanguard	Fidelity
Suggest %				
During Market plunge	90%	0%	0%	10%
After plunge	10%	60%	10%	20%

Explanation

- The above are suggestions only. If your broker offers similar ETFs, consider using them.

- Check out any restrictions of the ETFs.

- 4 ETFs (one actually is a money market fund) are enough for most starters. They are diversified, low-cost and you do not need balancing except during a market plunge (refer to the chapter on Detecting Market Plunges).

- The percentages are suggestions only. If you are less risk tolerant, allocate more to a money market fund, CD and/or bond ETF.

- Have at least 10% allocated to the money market fund. When there is a mild market dip, move the money market fund to the US equity fund. Move it back to money market when there is a mild market upsurge. If you do not have time to check the market, allocate this 10% to the bond ETF.

- When the market is risky, reduce stock equities (i.e. increase money market and bond allocations).

- The symbols for Fidelity ETFs are FSTMX, FSGDX and FBIDX.

- The symbols for Vanguard ETFs are VTSMX, VGTSX and VBMFX.

Filler

I got a call from Buffett asking me to lead their stock research.
I asked him why for a nobody; you may be asking the same question. No kidding.

He told me that he should have read my book Scoring Stocks to buy Apple instead of IBM in May, 2013. It would save his company millions of dollars minus $10 for my book. Not to mention the market timing technique that had worked in the last two major market plunges.

I told him, "OK, I'll beat your mediocre returns of the last 5 years."
He said, "You can do better than that and at least beat SPY. If you do so, no one will be that stupid to leave my fund and pay the hefty capital gain taxes."

I told him, "I cannot beat the market as you are the market especially after your expensive fees. In addition, I do not know how to avoid day traders from riding my wagon in trading. Also most of my big profits were made in small stocks that your fund cannot trade besides owning the company."

I woke up trembling. I'm glad it is only a nightmare.

Quick analysis of ETFs

Evaluate an ETF
ETFs are a basket of stocks according to the market, a specific sector, country or a specific theme.

Yahoo!Finance used to give the P/E of an ETF. Try to get it from ETFdb.com. Enter the symbol of the ETF such as XLU, and then select Valuation. If it is below 15 and above zero, it could be a value ETF. Also, if the current price is lower than its NAV, it is sold at a discount (or premium vice versa). Compare its YTD Return to SPY's.

Alternatively, get similar info from http://www.multpl.com/. In addition, this web site provides the following metrics: Shiller P/E, Price/Sales, and Price/Book.

From Finviz.com, enter the ETF symbol. If SMA-20%, SMA-50% and SMA-200% are all positive, most likely the ETF is in an uptrend. To illustrate, SMA-200 is Simple Moving Average for the last 200 trading sessions (no trading on weekends and specific holidays). The percent is how much the stock price of the ETF is above the SMA. If the percent is negative, it means the stock price is below the SMA.

If your average holding period of your stocks is about 50 days, SMA-50% is more appropriate to you.

If RSI(14) > 65, it is probably over-sold; if it is < 30, it is probably under-sold (indicating value).

In addition, ensure the ETF's average volume is high (I suggest more than 10,000 shares), the market cap is more than 300 M, and it has low fees. Most popular ETFs have these characteristics. Beginners should avoid leveraged ETFs.

How to determine if the sector has been recovered
It is easier to profit by following the uptrend of an ETF using the above info. It is hard to detect when the bottom of an ETF has been reached. If SMA-20%, SMA-50% and SMA-200% are all positive, most likely the ETF is in an uptrend or it has recovered. It does not always happen as predicted, so use stops to protect your investment.

An example
First, determine whether the market is risky. Most beginners should not invest in a risky market. Advanced investors can bet against the market or a specific sector by buying contra ETFs or puts.

Next, you want to limit the number of sector ETFs by selecting those that are either in an uptrend or hitting bottom (bottom is hard to predict). Personally I prefer sectors with long-term uptrends (indicated by articles found in many web sites including cnnfn.com and Seeking Alpha.

For illustration purposes only for deteriorating market conditions, I would select the following ETFs: SPY (simulating the market based on large companies) and XLP (consumer staples). XLP should perform better than XLY (consumer discretionary) during a recession as those products are the necessities.

Technical indicators such as SMA-50 (Simple Moving Average for the last 50 sessions), SMA-200 and RSI(14) are obtained from Finviz.com and the rest are obtained from Yahoo!Finance.com. After you buy the ETF, use a stop loss to protect your investment. For example, bio tech sector moved up for many months until it crashed in 2015. Change the stop loss value every month to protect your gains in this case.

As of 2/5/2016	SPY	XLP (staples)	XLY (discret.)
Price	190	50	71
NAV	192	50	73
• Technical			
SMA-50	-4%	0%	-7%
SMA-200	-6%	2%	-7%
RSI(14)	44	50	36
Other	Double bottom at $186		
• Fundamental			
P/E	17	20	19
Yield	2.1%	2.5%	1.5%
YTD return	-5%	0.5%	-5%
Net asset	174 B	9 B	10 B

Explanation
- The figures may not be identical among web sites due to the dates they are using.
- XLY has best discount among the 3 ETFs as most investors believe a recession is coming.
- XLP has less down trend among the 3 ETFs as expected.
- XLY is more undersold among the three as expected.
- Double bottom is a technical pattern that indicates the stock would surge upward.
- SPY has a better value according to its P/E.

- XLY's dividend is the least among the three as they have more tech companies in the ETF. They have to plow back the profits to research and development.
- XLP has the best YTD return among the three.
- As long as the asset is above 500 M (200 M for specialized ETFs), it is fine and all three pass this mark.

There are many metrics such as Debt/Equity not readily available from most web sites. Many sites list the top holdings of a specific ETF. Just average the metrics of the top ten or so of its stock holdings.

An example

This example evaluates RING, a gold miner, using ETFdb and Finviz that are free from the web. The data is from July, 6, 2020.

Bring up ETFdb and enter RING in the search. There are basic info that are important to me: Sector (gold miners), Asset Size (Large-Cap), Issuer (iShares), Inception (Jan. 31, 2012), Expense Ratio (0.39%) and Tax Form (1099).

They fit all my requirements. The expense ratio is higher than most ETFs that simulating an index such as SPY. I try to trade ETFs using Tax Form 1099 in my taxable accounts. The large cap created about 8 years ago by a reputable company are good.

Select "Dividend and Valuation". P/E of 17.39 is fine in a rank of 11 in 27 in similar group of ETFs. As in my books, I stated it is hard to evaluate miners. I buy this ETF primarily to fight the possibility of inflation and the potential depreciation of USD. The dividend rate of 0.52% (0.70% from Finviz) is in the low range of the scale; it is fine for me as dividend is not my concern.

There are more info from this web site. For simplicity, bring up Finviz:
- The short-term trend is up (SMA-20% = 8% and SMA-50% = 7%).
- The long-term trend is up (SMA-200% = 26%).
- It is close to overbought (RSI(14) = 64%; 65% to me is overbought).
- It is -4% from 52-w High. It has performed well from the YTD, Last Year, Last Quarter, Last Month and Last Week.
- It almost doubles in price from mid March this year.
- Avg. Vol. is fine.

From ETFdb, check the Holding. It has 39 stocks, so it is quite diversified for this industry. The two top holdings are NEM (19%) and ABX (18%), which is listed as GOLD in NYSX. I also consider to buy these two stocks in addition to RING. You can estimate the other metrics that are not available by averaging these two stocks. Here is my summary:

STOCK	NEM	GOLD
Forward P/E	20	25
Debt / Share	0.31	0.24
ROE	17%	22%
Sales Q/Q	43%	30%
EPS Q/Q	389%	254%
SMA50	2%	4%
RSI(14)	59%	60%
Insider Trans	-13%	N/A
Fidelity's Equity Summary Score	6.1	6.8

#Filler: Honey, my book can play music.
https://www.youtube.com/watch?v=HxGT5z6d-GA&list=PLMZa6mP7jZ2b1otqG4tfbgZpLEdh6YiNF
It may cut down commercials by casting it to TV.